PROGRAMMING IN
C++

Second Edition

Stephen C. Dewhurst • **Kathy T. Stark**

For book and bookstore information

http://www.prenhall.com
gopher to gopher.prenhall.com

Prentice Hall PTR
Upper Saddle River, New Jersey 07458

Editorial/production supervision: **Ann Sullivan**
Cover design: **Lundgren Graphics Ltd.**
Manufacturing buyer: **Alexis R. Heydt**
Acquisitions editor: **Gregory G. Doench**
Editorial assistant: **Meg Cowen**

Published by Prentice-Hall, Inc.
A Division of Simon & Schuster
Upper Saddle River, New Jersey 07458

The publisher offers discounts on this book when ordered in bulk quantities.
For more information, contact:

Corporate Sales Department
Prentice Hall PTR
1 Lake Street
Upper Saddle River, NJ 07458
Phone: 800-382-3419
Fax: 201-236-7141
email: corpsales@prenhall.com

Printed in the United States of America

10 9 8 7 6 5 4 3 2 1

ISBN   0-13-182718-9

Prentice-Hall International (UK) Limited, London
Prentice-Hall of Australia Pty. Limited, Sydney
Prentice-Hall Canada Inc., Toronto
Prentice-Hall Hispanoamericana, S.A., Mexico
Prentice-Hall of India Private Limited, New Delhi
Prentice-Hall of Japan, Inc., Tokyo
Simon & Schuster Asia Pte. Ltd., Singapore
Editora Prentice-Hall do Brasil, Ltda., Rio de Janeiro

Contents

Preface

Since the appearance of the first edition of this book in 1989, the C++ user community has continued to grow rapidly, new programming techniques have appeared on an almost daily basis, and the C++ language itself has continued to evolve. The "fertile exchange of ideas" that marked the state of the C++ community in 1989 continues unabated today, aided by the standardization process sponsored jointly by the American National Standards Institute and the International Standards Organization.

As book and compiler writers, our task is no easier now than it was in 1989. Faced with describing an evolving language, it is tempting to try to cover every detail of the emerging standard and every nuance of every major programming technique. Response to the first edition of *Programming in C++*, however, indicated that our decision to limit the discussion of language features in preference to discussion of programming issues was the correct one. Therefore, we continue to develop topics of programming paradigms and their supporting language features in parallel, in order to lead the reader beyond a simple syntactic understanding of the C++ language to its use as a flexible and effective programming tool.

We are indebted to many individuals—colleagues, students, and strangers—who contributed directly or indirectly to this second edition. Special thanks are given to Christopher Aoki for his support, patience, and persistent encouragement. Sarah Hewins lent her sharp eye and sharper commentary to various drafts of the manuscript; her support and impatience were much appreciated.

Clovis Tondo has been a driving force behind the production of this second edition. Over a period of years he has provided motivation, encouragement, technical review, and an occasional swift kick to keep us moving.

Hiroshi Koyama, who translated the first edition into Japanese, contributed the material and examples in Chapter 1 on wide characters and wide-character strings, and provided aid as a reviewer. We thank Hiroshi for his contributions as well as his encouragement through the seasons of writing.

S.C.D.

K.T.S.

Preface to the First Edition

C++ has become an increasingly popular programming language. Its appeal is due not only to the popularity of its parent language C, but also to its data abstraction and object-oriented features. The development of C++ has been marked by an active dialog among a community of users who contributed to the language's formation with a fertile exchange of ideas. The result is that C++ is a language with a rich range of features that supports a variety of programming methods and techniques.

The C++ language can best be understood by observing how the language features work together in writing programs. As both users and implementors of C++ at a time when the language was being formed, we had the unusual opportunity to see why certain language features were developed and to participate in their refinement through implementation and use. In this book, we hope to share our understanding and appreciation of C++ as a programming tool.

We wrote this book at a time when C++ was still evolving. Our presentation of C++ tries to avoid details that might cause confusion among users of different versions of the language, however, new features like multiple inheritance, and refinements to the language definition and implementation might make the language we present somewhat different from the implementation the reader has available. We did not intend to write a language reference manual or a description of a particular implementation. We did intend to guide our readers beyond the details of the features to general concepts of program design that help programmers use C++ effectively.

This book has benefited by contributions made by many of those who participated in the development of C++. We gratefully acknowledge the contributions made by many individuals to the development of C++ programming methodologies and techniques. Their thoughts have influenced us greatly, and many of their ideas have found their way into this book: Tom

Cargill, Jim Coplien, Keith Gorlen, Bill Hopkins, Andy Koenig, Jerry Schwarz, and Jon Shopiro are chief among these pioneers. We would also like to thank our colleagues Laura Eaves, Phil Brown, and Stan Lippman, who worked with us in the development of a C++ compiler; Sarah Hewins, Bob Wilson, and Wayne Wolf, who reviewed various drafts of the manuscript; and Jeff Monin, who lent us his time and expertise at several key points. John Wait of Prentice-Hall provided motivation and guidance for this project from start to finish.

To Brian Kernighan our debt is of an entirely different order. Brian persevered through many versions of the manuscript, guiding us from obscurity towards clarity. That we may not have completed the journey reflects more on our stubbornness than his perseverance and persuasion.

Bjarne Stroustrup not only originated C++ and evolved it into a rich programming language, but he was willing to argue about it on the way. We thank Bjarne for many valuable discussions and disputations, as well as for his support for this project.

S.C.D.

K.T.S.

CHAPTER 0: **Introduction**

C++ is a general purpose programming language derived from C. It adds to its parent language a number of features, the most important of which are those supporting data abstraction and object-oriented programming. C++ retains most of its C heritage, and has adopted C's basic data types, operations, statement syntax, and program structure. Added features enhance the C-like parts of the language as well as support new programming techniques.

Programming languages are not produced by spontaneous generation, but are, in effect, generated by shifts in the way people think about the process of programming. Generalized and codified, these thought processes achieve the status of paradigms, and new languages are created to support them. Programming paradigms, then, are models that provide sets of techniques to be applied when designing and implementing programs. These techniques address issues such as how a design relates to a programming problem, the use of abstraction, and program organization. A language supports a particular paradigm if the features of that language make it easy to apply the techniques of that model. The features of C++ allow a range of techniques without constraining the user to any one paradigm.

Most books on programming languages teach the language features but abandon the reader to discover alone the process of programming in the language. For a language like C++, which is significantly richer than most languages with which the reader may be familiar, this approach is unsatisfactory. This book is about how to *program* using C++. We discuss the details of how to use C++ features as well as how to apply paradigms in design and implementation.

Our presentation progressively develops concepts in order to place both programming paradigms and language features in context. Although we cover most features, we do not present a minutely detailed description of the language. We assume our readers are experienced programmers familiar with

1

C, and we go into the most detail in presenting what the C programmer finds new when programming in C++.

0.1 The C++ Language

The major addition C++ makes to C is the introduction of class types. Classes allow a user to define aggregate data types that include not only data members but also functions that operate on the type. Data hiding in classes provides the mechanism for data abstraction. Class inheritance extends data abstraction to object-oriented programming. Templates allow classes to be parameterized into generic types. User-defined operator functions and conversions enable classes to be integrated into the existing type system by allowing class type operands in expressions and conversions among class and nonclass types.

Classes include features that enable memory management to be built into dynamic data structures. The language also provides general dynamic allocation and deallocation operators. This combination allows a programmer to tailor a memory management scheme to a specific application or problem domain.

Besides the features that support techniques for building data structures, there are also those that enhance the use of functions. All C++ function declarations must include argument type information. This allows argument type checking and function overloading. Function argument declarations may also include default values for arguments not given in a function call. Reference types in C++ allow arguments to be passed by reference as well as by value. Exceptions provide an error return mechanism in cases where abnormal conditions require special handling.

0.2 Programming Paradigms

Programming paradigms are models of how to design and implement programs. Different models result in different techniques. That the techniques are different does not imply they are in conflict, and various techniques can be seen to complement one another. What programming models seem to have in common are the notions that the design should be based on abstractions that correspond to elements in the programming problem, and that the implementation should be a collection of modules, preferably reusable ones. They differ in how to form the abstractions and what constitutes a module.

The well-established methods of procedural programming are based on a model of building a program as a collection of functions. The techniques provide guidance on how to design, organize, and implement the functions that make up a program. The design method of functional decomposition identifies the functions that serve as the abstract operations that solve a programming problem. File organization allows functions to be grouped in separate modules; structured programming techniques make the implementation of a function readable and maintainable.

Data abstraction focuses on the data structures neglected by procedure-oriented techniques. The model of data abstraction is that a data structure should be defined by the operations on it rather than by the structure of its implementation. The technique used for data abstraction is to encapsulate a data structure in an abstract data type. Access to the structure is provided through a set of operations that are part of the type. Data abstraction complements the procedural programming view of functions as abstract operations because neither abstraction is complete without the other.

Object-oriented programming is based on a model of building programs as a collection of abstract data type instances. Object-oriented design identifies the types that represent objects in the programming problem and the relationships among those types. The operations in the object types are, like the functions in the procedural programming model, the abstract operations that solve the problem. The object type serves as a module that can be reused for solving another problem in the same domain.

No single paradigm is suitable for solving all programming problems well. Programming requires engineering expertise but is not yet a science. Programming techniques need to be applied flexibly, with an eye to how well they suit the problem at hand. Blind application of the currently most popular paradigm is never a substitute for careful examination and thoughtful abstraction of a problem. A major goal of this book is to encourage the reader to think, both critically and flexibly, about problems in program design and implementation.

0.3 Book Organization

We intend to teach the reader how to design and implement programs using C++. This book's organization interweaves presentation of the C++ language with discussion of the techniques and paradigms for which the features were designed. We start with the data types and operations of the language, proceed through ways of organizing data structures and operations into programs, and end with the advanced topics of memory management and library design.

One view of programs is that they describe a sequence of operations on data, and so the C++ data types and operations are presented in Chapter 1. The language features adopted from C can be seen to provide abstract data types and operations, such as numbers and arithmetic operations. User-defined class types are presented as a means of adding both data types and operations to the language.

Chapter 2 discusses procedural programming techniques for organizing sequences of operations into functions. Functional decomposition and structured programming are covered as design paradigms, along with the supporting language features of scope and linkage of names, parameter passing by value and reference, overloading of function names, default arguments, function templates, and inline functions.

Chapter 3 covers the basic features of C++ classes. This straightforward presentation of language features provides the underpinnings on which much of the rest of the book is based. We cover data and function members, constructors and destructors, operator overloading, and protection.

Chapter 4 discusses the use of classes for data abstraction. We show how to develop a new data type, using the facilities provided by classes to make the implementation secure and maintainable, and how to define conversions and operations that integrate the new type into the existing type system.

Chapter 5 covers class inheritance, a feature that allows a new class type to be defined in terms of existing class types. Inheritance can be used to modify an existing abstract data type, create hierarchical collections of related abstract types, combine the properties of unrelated types, and provide flexible runtime binding of function calls.

Chapter 6 applies the use of data abstraction and inheritance to object-oriented programming design. We present guidelines for designing and organizing a program as object type modules and demonstrate the dynamic object-oriented programming style.

Chapter 7 presents the memory management features of C++. Efficient and maintainable memory management schemes can be developed and tailored for general use, for a given library or class type, or for a specific application.

In Chapter 8 we discuss the design and use of libraries as collections of reusable software modules. We show how to design libraries so that they are extensible and modifiable by their users without affecting the library source code.

The last section of each chapter contains exercises. Those marked with a † have solutions given in the Appendix.

We relate the details of the C++ language to larger problems of software design and engineering. We hope our readers learn not only how to use C++ effectively as a programming tool, but are also stimulated to think in new ways about the process of designing and implementing programs.

CHAPTER 1: Data Types and Operations

The C++ type system consists of basic language-defined types, user-defined class types, and types that can be derived from the basic and class types. The language provides operations and standard conversions for the built-in types. Class types can also have operations and conversions defined for them, thus allowing classes to be used as consistent extensions of the predefined type system.

The built-in data types in C++ can be interpreted as abstract concepts, such as numbers or boolean values, or according to their representation in the computer as a sequence of bits. The interpretation depends on the operations used to manipulate the values of the different types. The arithmetic and logical operators give results that preserve the mathematical and logical interpretations of the types. Other operators give results that depend on and reveal the bit representation.

1.1 Numeric Types

C++ has both integer and floating point numeric types. The language provides arithmetic operators that are overloaded to work with both integer and floating point values, and defines conversions among the numeric types. Overloaded operators are those operators for which the same symbol represents more than one distinct implementation of an operation. The numeric types, when used with arithmetic operators, are interpreted as representations of numbers.

The following program performs a calculation using numeric variables and values with arithmetic operators. To represent integers, `int` values are used; `double` floating point values are used to represent real numbers.

```
#include <stdio.h>

main() {
/*
    Distance of a falling object from the point of its
    release at each of the first 10 seconds of its fall,
    in meters
*/
    const double g = 9.80; // acceleration from gravity

    for( int t = 1; t <= 10; t++ ) {
        double distance = g * t * t / 2;
        printf( "\t%2d %7.2f\n", t, distance );
    }
}
```

The program prints out the distance an object has fallen at each of the first ten
seconds after being dropped:

```
 1     4.90
 2    19.60
 3    44.10
 4    78.40
 5   122.50
 6   176.40
 7   240.10
 8   313.60
 9   396.90
10   490.00
```

The expression calculating the distance mixes `double` and `int` type
operands. The result is a `double` value that is stored in the `double` variable `distance`.

```
    double distance = g * t * t / 2;
```

Although both `t` and 2 have type `int`, the calculation is done completely
with floating point operations. Since `g` has type `double`, and the multiplica-
tions and division group left to right, each operator in the calculation has at
least one `double` operand that forces the conversion of the `int` operand to
match it.

The arithmetic operators are overloaded for the numeric types. The types
of the operands determine whether an integer or floating point operation is
performed. If the expression is changed so that the operations are done in a

different order, the types of some of the operations may also change.

```
distance = g * ( t * t / 2 );
```

With parentheses forcing the grouping of the integer operands, there is an integer multiplication of t by t producing an int result. The division is also applied to int operands. The integer division has an int type result; when t is odd, the fractional part of the result is lost, and this calculation produces different results from the previous one with floating point operations. Using a floating point literal for the divisor forces the operation to be floating point division, and the result returns to the previous accuracy.

```
distance = g * ( t * t / 2.0 );
```

For an overloaded operator, the types of the operands affect which implementation of the operator is used to perform the operation.

The arithmetic operators are defined to work for operands of several numeric types. The unary arithmetic operators are increment ++, decrement --, negation -, and no-op +. The binary arithmetic operators are multiplication *, division /, addition +, and subtraction -. In addition, the remainder operator % works only on integer operands.

The increment and decrement operators have the side effect of changing the value of the object that is their operand. They can be used in either prefix or postfix form with different results. In the prefix form, the result of the expression is that of the object after it was incremented or decremented. In the postfix form, the expression value is that of the object before it is changed. Other arithmetic operators do not change the value of their operands.

Unary operators have higher precedence than binary operators. The multiplicative binary operators *, /, and % have higher precedence than the additive operators + and -.

The integer types are char, short, int, and long. Each type can represent at least the range of values as the previous type on the list, so each can be thought of as larger or equal in size to the preceding type. The integer types come in both signed and unsigned versions. In declarations, short, int, and long type specifiers mean the signed versions of these types unless unsigned is explicitly specified. When different types of integer operands are combined in an expression, they are converted to be the same type. Operands of type char and short are always converted at least to int. Other conversions are always to the larger of the operand types.

Conversions are only made to the `unsigned` version of a type if one operand type is `unsigned` and larger or equal in size to the other operand type. There are versions of C++ that support a `long long` type for holding very large integer values such as offsets in large capacity storage devices.

The floating point types are `float`, `double`, and `long double`. Each type can represent at least the set of values of the previous type on the list, so each can be thought of as containing the preceding type. When different floating point types are combined as operands in an arithmetic expression, the smaller-sized operand is converted to the same type as the other operand. When floating point and integer operands are combined, the integer is converted to the same type as the floating point operand.

Any numeric value can be assigned to an object of any other numeric type. The value is then converted to the type on the left-hand side of the assignment.

```
double d;
d = 42;
```

The conversion may result in loss of part of the value.

```
int i;
i = 3.1415;
char c;
c = 777;
```

In the above, `i` is given the value 3. The value `777` is probably too large to be represented in a `char`, so the value of `c` after the assignment depends on how a particular implementation handles the conversion from the larger to smaller sized integer type.

Conversion operators, or *casts*, can be used for explicit conversions. For example, in the following, the `int` value of `count` is explicitly converted to `double`.

```
int count = 1066, total = 1337;
double ratio;

ratio = double( count ) / total;
```

This example uses a function-call style cast:

```
double( count )
```

An alternative form of the same cast operation is:

```
( double )count
```

The function-call form is usually considered the clearer style in simple conversion expressions.

Numeric values can be directly represented in a program as numeric literals. Floating point literals may have a decimal point and a fractional part, as well as an exponent:

```
9.80
0.98e1
98e-1
```

These literals all represent the same value and have type `double`. For values of different floating point types, the suffix L or l indicates `long double`, and F or f indicates `float`.

```
0.98e1L
9.80f
```

Integer literals have type `int` unless their value is too large to be contained in an `int` or their type is indicated with a suffix. A literal value too large to be represented as an `int` may have type `long`. A suffix L or l indicates a `long`, and U or u indicates `unsigned`. These suffixes may be combined:

```
1642UL
```

An octal literal is indicated with a 0 first digit:

```
0777
```

A hexadecimal literal is indicated with a leading 0x or 0X. The letters in hexadecimal literals can be either upper or lower case.

```
0x1ff
0X1fF
```

Numeric values may also be represented symbolically by using a `const` with an initializing value.

```
const double g = 9.80;
```

Since the `const` indicates that the value of g cannot be changed, the identifier always represents its initial value 9.80.

Integer values may also be represented symbolically by members of `enum` lists. If not otherwise initialized, the `enum` members have successive integral values, with the first one having the value 0.

```
enum { MON, TUES, WED, THUR, FRI, SAT, SUN };
```

Here, `FRI` has the value 4. When `enum` members are explicitly initialized, uninitialized members of the list have values that are one more than the previous value on the list.

```
enum { MON = 1, TUES, WED, THUR, FRI, SAT = -1, SUN };
```

In this case, the value of `FRI` is 5, and the value of `SUN` is 0.

An `enum` may be declared with a tag that becomes the name of an integral type.

```
enum Day { MON, TUES, WED, THUR, FRI, SAT, SUN };
```

A variable declared as an `enum` type can only be assigned values of the same type.

```
Day aday;

aday = FRI;   // OK FRI is a value of type Day
aday = 18;    // error! assignment of an int to a Day
aday = 4;     // error! FRI has value 4, but 4 is an int
```

However, an `enum` type value is automatically converted to `int` in expressions. An `int` may be converted to an `enum`, but the integer should be in the range of `enum` values for correct results.

```
aday = Day(4);   // OK FRI has value 4
aday = Day(18);  // undefined behavior! program error
```

1.2 Characters

C++ has two different character types `char` and `wchar_t`. These are integral types that can be used in a program to hold the codes corresponding to characters in a given character set.

C++ uses a Latin character set represented by code values that can be contained in a `char` data type. The C++ character set is suitable for the representation of most American-English text. European, and other alphabets with relatively small numbers of characters, are also represented with single byte, `char` type encodings.

Members of Japanese, Chinese, and Korean character sets, however, are encoded in sequences of one, two, or more bytes, with different sized values in one set. In C++, the multibyte encodings of these character sets can be converted to values of the distinct `wchar_t`, or "wide character," type; `wchar_t` representations all have the same size for easy manipulation within a program.

Although C++ is based on English, characters from the local character sets are allowed in comments, included file names, and as character literals. For example, in a Japanese locale the following is allowed:

```
#include "ヘッダ.h"
// これは日本語のコメントです.
```

Character literals, which are characters or escape sequences in single quotes, provide a convenient representation of character values:

```
char w = 'w';
char newline = '\n';
char tab = '\t';
char null = '\0';
char bell = '\007';
```

Wide character literals are indicated by a `L` prefix:

```
wchar_t wc = L'あ';
```

Wide character values can also be indicated with escape sequences:

```
wchar_t wchar_null = L'\0';
```

Escape sequences that start with \ followed by up to three octal digits give the character value as an octal number instead of as a symbol. Hexadecimal numbers may also be used in escape sequences starting \x.

The C++ character code values are always positive, even when they are contained in a `signed char`. They can also be used as integer operands in expressions:

```
char digit = '9';
int value = digit - '0';
```

Arithmetic calculations on character values usually assume a standard character encoding. The above example relies on ASCII code values for correctness.

The wide character code values used within C++ are typically different from the multibyte encodings of Japanese, Chinese, and Korean characters stored in text files. There are standard library functions `mbtowc`, and `wctomb`, declared in the header file `stdlib.h` for converting between the wide character and multibyte encodings. The behavior of these functions are locale- and implementation-specific.

1.3 Scalar Types with Relational and Logical Operators

In C++, scalar types, like integers, work as boolean types with zero representing the value false and any nonzero value representing true. Pointers are also scalar types and are described later in this chapter. The relational operators are used to compare values and return true or false in the form of an integer value of 1 or 0. The logical operators work on scalar operands interpreted as true or false and likewise return 1 or 0.

Relational operators produce `int` results of either 1 or 0. The example in the previous section calculating the distance traveled during a fall uses a relational expression to control the loop.

```
for( int t = 1; t <= 10; t++ ) {
    // etc.
}
```

To highlight the control condition, we will rewrite the `for` loop as an equivalent `while` loop.

```
int t = 1;
while( t <= 10 ) {
    // etc.
    t++;
}
```

The loop body executes as long as the condition `t  <=  10` does not evaluate to 0. The expression evaluates to 1 as long as t is less than or equal to 10 so the loop executes for values of t from 1 to 10.

The relational operators are less than <, greater than >, less than or equal to <= and greater than or equal to >=. There are also the equality operators equal to == and not equal to !=. These operators are overloaded for integer and floating point, as well as pointer operands, but always produce an `int` result of 1 or 0.

Since any nonzero value represents true, any expression can serve as a condition, not just those that evaluate to 1 or 0. For example:

```
int t = 11;
while( --t ) {
    // etc.
}
```

The loop body executes for values of t from 10 to 1.

It is generally good practice to put explicit comparisons in loop controls. For example:

```
while( --t > 0 ) {
    // etc.
}
```

This loop will not execute if the value of t is initially zero or negative.

The logical operators are logical-and &&, logical-or ||, and logical-not !. An expression with the unary operator ! evaluates to 0 if its operand is nonzero and 1 otherwise. For example, the following sets a previously zero valued variable:

```
if( !p )  // i.e. if( p == 0 )
    p = get_a_val();
```

Expressions using || evaluate to 0 if both operands are 0 and 1 otherwise. In the following example, the function error is called only if the value of x is not in the range 0 to 10.

```
if( x < 0 || x > 10 )
    error("value outside range");
```

An && expression evaluates to 1 if both operands are nonzero and 0 otherwise. The following checks the same condition as the previous example using a different logical expression:

```
if( !( x >= 0 && x <= 10 ) )
    error("value outside range");
```

The first expression is preferable to the second because it is easier to understand.

The second operand of `&&` and `||` is evaluated only if needed to determine the result of the expression. If the first operand of an `||` expression evaluates to nonzero, the result is 1 regardless of the value of the second operand. Likewise, if the first operand of an `&&` expression evaluates to 0, the second operand is not evaluated, and the result of the expression is 0. For example, in the following, if b has the value 0, the equality expression is not evaluated and the division subexpression will likewise be bypassed.

```
if( b && a/b == c ) {
    // etc.
}
```

The use of `&&` checks that b is not 0 and thus avoids the possibility of a division by 0. It is an error to rely on the evaluation of the second argument of `&&` or `||` for side effects. In the following, the function f may not be called if a is nonzero.

```
if( a || f() ) {
    // ERROR! if code relies on a side-effect of f()
}
```

1.4   Nonabstract Operations

C++ has a number of operations that allow a programmer to bypass abstract interpretations of types and get at their machine representation.

Integer types are implemented on a computer as bit sequences of different lengths. When integers are used with arithmetic, relational, or logical operators, their values are interpreted abstractly as numbers, or as true or false, and the details of the bit representation can largely be ignored by the programmer. Sometimes, however, the programmer wants to deal with the bits.

Below is a string hash function originated by Peter Weinberger. A hash function calculates a numeric value from a character string and is used to determine a storage location for information keyed on the string. The parameter is a pointer to a sequence of characters that are used as numeric values in the calculation. The variable `hash` is manipulated as a sequence of 32 bits until it is used as a numeric value in taking the remainder of its division by `prime`.

```
int
hashpjw( char *s ) {
    const prime = 211;
    unsigned hash = 0, g;

    for( char *p = s; *p ; p++ ) {
        hash = ( hash << 4 ) + *p;
        // assumes 32 bit int size
        if( g = hash & 0xf0000000 ) {
            hash ^= g >> 24;
            hash ^= g;
        }
    }
    return hash % prime;
}
```

The bitwise operators used above are left shift <<, right shift >>, bitwise-and &, and bitwise-exclusive-or ^. Bitwise-inclusive-or | and the unary bitwise-complement ~ are also available.

The ^ operator is used in the example in the form of an assignment operator ^=. The expression

```
        hash ^= g;
```

is equivalent to

```
        hash = hash ^ g;
```

The binary operators *, /, %, |, -, <<, >>, &, ^, and | can all be combined with assignment in the same way.

The `sizeof` operator gives the number of bytes used to represent a type. For example the result of

```
    sizeof( int )
```

is the number of bytes used to represent an `int`. The value of

```
    sizeof( char )
```

is always 1. When the operand is an expression instead of a type, the result is the size of the type of the expression. A major use of this operator—determining the space needed for dynamic creation of an object—has been incorporated into the C++ memory management operators **new** and

delete. With these operators taking care of the mechanics of space allocation, a programmer will rarely need to know the size of a type representation.

1.5 User-Defined Types

Class types can be defined by the user to extend the basic C++ type system. Operations and conversions can be defined for class types so that they
can be used in combination with other types.

The following is a program that calculates the voltage of an AC electrical
circuit containing an inductor, a resistor, and a capacitor using the formula
$Z = R + j\omega L + 1/(j\omega C)$ for impedance and $V = ZI$ for voltage. The
voltage, current, and impedance of AC circuits have two components that are
represented by the real and imaginary parts of a complex number. There is no
language-defined complex number type in C++. The program uses a user-
defined class type to represent complex number values.

```
#include "complex.h"

main() {
/*
   calculate voltage of an AC circuit
*/
   const complex j( 0, 1 );  // imaginary 1
   const double pi = 3.1415926535897931;

   double
      L = .03,  // inductance, in henries
      R = 5000,    // resistance, in ohms
      C = .02,  // capacitance, in farads
      freq = 60,   // frequency in hertz
      omega = 2 * pi * freq;
             // frequency in radians/sec
   complex
      I = 12,   // current
      Z,        // impedance
      V;        // voltage
```

```
    Z = R + j * omega * L + 1/( j * omega * C );
    V = Z * I;
    V.print();
}
```

The output of the program is

```
    ( 60000.00, 134.13 )
```

The header file `complex.h` contains the definition of the class type `complex` that implements the mathematical notion of complex numbers. An abridged version of `class complex` is used for the example.

```
class complex {
    double re, im;
  public:
    complex( double r = 0, double i = 0 )
        { re = r; im = i; }
    void print();
    friend complex operator +( complex, complex );
    friend complex operator *( complex, complex );
    friend complex operator /( complex, complex );
};
```

The class definition contains the declarations of members as well as the declaration of `friend` functions; these latter have special access to members of the class. The members declared after the `public` label are accessible without restriction, whereas the private members, `re` and `im`, can only be accessed by member and friend functions. The data member representation of `complex` is hidden in the private part of the class so that the type is only usable through the publicly available functions.

The member function with the same name as the class is a *constructor*. The constructor is used to create and initialize `complex` objects, or to convert values of other types to the class type. This constructor is declared with default argument values; therefore, it can be invoked with zero, one, or two arguments, with the default arguments being filled in when needed. The declaration

```
    const complex j( 0, 1 );
```

has an initializer that provides both constructor arguments, with the real and imaginary parts of j being set to 0 and 1 respectively. The declaration

```
complex I = 12;
```

is equivalent to

```
complex I( 12, 0 );
```

The default argument fills in 0 for the argument that sets the imaginary part of I. Both Z and V are initialized with the default constructor arguments, because no other initial values are indicated in their declarations.

The other functions declared in class complex are defined outside the class:

```
void
complex::print() {
    printf("( %5.2f, %5.2f )\n", re, im );
}

complex
operator +( complex a1, complex a2 ) {
    return complex( a1.re + a2.re, a1.im + a2.im );
}

complex
operator *( complex a1, complex a2 )
{
    return complex(a1.re * a2.re - a1.im * a2.im,
            a1.re * a2.im + a1.im * a2.re);
}

complex
operator /( complex a1, complex a2 )
{
    double r = a2.re;    /* (r,i) */
    double i = a2.im;
    double ti;           /* (tr,ti) */
    double tr;

    tr = r < 0? -r : r;
    ti = i < 0? -i : i;
```

```
    if( tr <= ti ) {
        ti = r/i;
        tr = i * (1 + ti*ti);
        r = a1.re;
        i = a1.im;
    }
    else {
        ti = -i/r;
        tr = r * (1 + ti*ti);
        r = -a1.im;
        i = a1.re;
    }
    return complex( (r*ti + i)/tr, (i*ti - r)/tr );
}
```

The member function `print` is used in the example to print the resulting value of V.

```
    V.print();
```

As a member function, `print` can access all the other members of the class without restriction. It formats and prints the `re` and `im` members of the `complex` object for which it is called.

The operator functions are declared as `friend` inside `class complex`. Friend functions are not members of the class, but like member functions they are allowed access to private members of a `complex` object. The operator functions implement arithmetic operations for `complex` values and allow `complex` operands in expressions with infix notation.

```
    Z = R + j * omega * L + 1/( j * omega * C );
```

The expression that calculates impedance mixes `int`, `double`, and `complex` operands. When an `int` or `double` operand is used with a `complex` one, the constructor is automatically applied to convert the operand to `complex` before the operator function is called with the operands as arguments. Predefined conversions between built-in types are applied to get the correct constructor argument types, so the single constructor serves to convert both `int` and `double` operands. When the `complex` constructor is used in conversions, the default value is filled in as the second argument.

With the hidden representation and user-defined operators and conversions, `class complex` is an abstract numeric type that combines naturally with the predefined numeric types.

1.6 Pointers and Arrays

Pointers and arrays are derived from other types. Pointer types represent the addresses of objects of another type. They are used to keep track of dynamically allocated objects, for flexibility in data structures, and with pointer arithmetic operators to access elements of arrays. Array types represent a sequence of elements of a particular type and have many uses as aggregate data structures. One standard use of arrays is as strings, which are sequences of characters.

Pointer types are indicated by using the type modifier * along with other type information in declarations. The same symbol is used for the pointer dereference operator, which returns the object to which the pointer refers. The result of a dereference can be used for the value of the object or on the left-hand side of an assignment.

```
int *p;       // p is a pointer to int
int i = 33;
p = &i;       // p set to point to i
*p = *p + 1; // i set to 34
```

The & operator returns the address of the object that is its operand. Address values have the type pointer-to-object-type. In the above example, the expression &i has the type pointer-to-int.

The dynamic allocation operator `new` creates an object having a type indicated by its operand and returns a pointer to the new object. An object created by `new` can be destroyed using operator `delete`, which takes as its operand a pointer to the doomed object.

```
int *p = 0;

if( !p )
    p = new int;

delete p;
p = 0;
```

The code fragment above declares a pointer and initializes it to 0, which is the special null pointer value and an invalid address. The pointer is checked to see if it has been set, and if not, it is given the address of a newly created object. The object is then deleted, and the pointer is reset to null. The combination of pointers, the use of null pointers as flags, and the allocation and deallocation of objects with operators `new` and `delete` are the rudiments for building dynamic data structures in C++.

There are no automatic conversions among pointer types except in limited cases in assignment and initialization. There is a special `void *` pointer type that will hold a pointer value of any type. One can think of `void *` as a pointer-to-anything type. Any other pointer type is automatically converted to match a `void *` in an assignment or initialization.

```
int *ip;
void *vp = ip;
double *dp;
vp = dp;
ip = (int *)vp; // not a good idea
```

A `void *` is only converted to another type of pointer if the programmer explicitly requests it with a cast. Such an explicit conversion is risky because it bypasses the type checking that ensures that the pointed-to object is interpreted in a consistent way. There are automatic conversions among pointers to related class types. These are discussed in Chapter 5.

An array is a sequence of contiguously allocated elements of the same type. The addresses of the elements in an array can be calculated from those of other elements using arithmetic operations overloaded for pointer operands. A loop that sequences through the elements of a string demonstrates a use of pointer arithmetic:

```
for( char *p = s; *p ; p++ ) {
    // etc.
```

In this example, `s` is an array of `char`, which represents a string. The pointer `p` is initialized to point to the first element in the array and then incremented to point to successive elements until one of the elements is 0. The string is conventionally terminated by a 0 element.

Both increment ++ and decrement -- operators work on pointer operands whose values are assumed to be the addresses of array elements. Increment changes the pointer to refer to the next element in the array, and decrement changes it to refer to the previous element.

The binary operators addition + and subtraction – are defined to work on one pointer operand and one integer operand. For subtraction, the integer must be the second operand. Again, the pointers are assumed to be the addresses of array elements. The results of the operations are addresses of other array elements. For example, the following addition adjusts p to point to the third element past the one to which it originally pointed.

```
p += 3;
```

The following subtraction sets p to the second element before the original one.

```
p -= 2;
```

Subtraction is also defined to work on two pointer operands that are the addresses of elements in the same array. The result is an integer value that is the number of elements between the array locations referred to by the pointers.

An array type is indicated with the type modifier [ ]. In an array declaration, the braces contain an integer constant expression that specifies the number of elements in the array. For example,

```
char buffer[100];
```

declares an array of 100 char elements. The name buffer represents the address of the first element in the array. This name can be used with the pointer arithmetic operations to access the elements of the array. The following loop zeros out the elements of buffer.

```
for( int i = 0; i < 100; i++ )
    *( buffer + i ) = 0;
```

A pointer expression can be used to access array elements. In the following, p is initially set to the address of the first element of buffer and then used to copy the first twenty elements into another array called name.

```
char name[21];

p = buffer;
for( i = 0;  i < 20;  i++ )
    name[i] = *p++;
name[i] = '\0'; // set string terminator
```

The subscript operator `[]` provides a shorthand expression for the pointer operations used to access array elements. The subscript expression

```
name[i]
```

is the same as

```
*(name + i)
```

The subscript operator can be used with any pointer operand, not just with array names. The following sets the location before p to null:

```
p[-1] = '\0';
```

The basic representation of a string in C++ is a sequence of character values in a `char` array with a terminating 0 element. Wide character strings are similarly formed with a `wchar_t` array. String literals provide a way of representing such arrays. A string literal is a sequence of characters or escape sequences surrounded by double quotes:

```
"This is a string literal\n"
```

Wide character string literals are indicated with a preceding L.

```
wchar_t* wcs = L"漢字ABC";
```

The value of a string literal is a pointer to the first element of an array of the character type. The size of the array is one more than the number of characters between the double quotes. Each array element has the value of the corresponding character in the literal. The last element in the array has the value 0.

1.7 References

Reference types establish aliases for objects. They are most often used as function parameter types in order to pass arguments by reference instead of by value.

A reference type is indicated in a declaration by using the modifier & in the same way as a pointer modifier. A reference must have an initializer. Once the reference is initialized, its use produces the same results as if the aliased object were used directly. The major use of references is for formal parameter types. In order to demonstrate how references work, we first show them in nonparameter declarations.

To establish an alias, the initializer must be the name of an object of the type that is referenced.

```
int i;
int &ir = i;
```

This establishes `ir` as an alias for `i`. Assignment to and use of `ir` produces the same results as assignment to and use of `i`.

```
ir = 3;        // i gets the value 3
int j;
int *ip;
j = i * ir;  // j gets the value 9
ip = &ir; // ip gets the address of i
```

Once the initializer establishes the object that the reference aliases, it cannot be changed. Current C++ compilers will give an error if a reference initializer is not of the correct type to establish an alias.

In old versions of C++, if the initializer for the reference is not of the right type, an anonymous object is created for which the reference becomes an alias. The initializer is converted and its value is then used to set the value of the anonymous object.

```
double d;
int &ir = d; // anonymous int object created
ir = 3.0;    // d is not changed!
```

An anonymous object may also be created to initialize a reference when the initializer is not an object.

```
int &ir = 3; // anonymous object gets value 3
```

The creation of an anonymous object to initialize a reference can be a difficult to detect program error. In most older implementations that accept such initializations the compiler produces a warning.

A major use of reference type parameters is to allow a function to set the value of its actual arguments. In this case, references are used to establish aliases for the arguments within the function, implementing read/write or write-only parameters.

```
void input( int &, int &, int & );
int a, b, c;

input( a, b, c );   // set argument values
```

If an argument conversion causes a reference parameter to be initialized with an anonymous temporary object, the function results set through the reference parameter become inaccessible to the rest of the program.

```
double d;
input( a, b, d );   // error! d not changed by input
```

For this reason, initialization of a reference with anything but a properly typed, named object is an error in current versions of C++. Pointer parameters can also be used to change objects external to the function, but address and pointer operations are then needed in manipulating arguments and parameters. Reference parameters that establish aliases provide a convenient alternative to pointer arguments.

Another use of reference parameters is to avoid the overhead of initializing parameters with argument values. This is most important for class parameters in which the argument values might actually be rather large data structures.

```
class List {
    // list of up to 100 int elements
    int size;
    int elements[100];
  public:
    int &item( int );
    // ...
} list;

void output( List & ); // don't copy list value
```

In this example, output will use the List argument directly without copying its value, thus avoiding the overhead of reproducing the array of elements.

A return type can be a reference, allowing the function to be used on the left-hand-side of an assignment. The member function List::item(), above, returns a reference to an element of the list:

```
int &
List::item( int ix ) {
    // ... check range of ix
    return elements[ix];
};
```

This one function can now be used both to access and to set list elements.

```
int i = list.item(3);  // get element value
list.item(12) = 6;  // set element through the reference
```

1.8 Const Qualified Types

The const type qualifier indicates that an object of the type cannot have its value changed, either directly or through a pointer. As mentioned earlier in this chapter, this property allows a const to be a symbolic representation of its initializing value.

Reference parameters that are used to prevent argument copying and are not intended to change arguments can be declared const to ensure that they do not. The const qualifier prevents the actual parameters from being altered within the function.

A const qualified reference parameter can be initialized with an anonymous object created by a conversion. This allows conversions to be performed to match arguments to reference parameters in the same way as non-reference parameters. For example, we could change our complex operator functions so they do not copy complex arguments but still allow conversions for other numeric arguments:

```
class complex {
    // etc.
    friend complex
    operator *( const complex &, const complex & );
};

complex V, Z;
// etc.

V = Z * 12;
```

The expression Z*12 is a call to the complex operator * function with the arguments Z and an anonymous complex object initialized with 12. These objects initialize the `const` qualified reference parameters and so argument passing overhead is reduced without preventing conversions in mixed type expressions.

In a pointer declaration, the position of `const` indicates whether it is the pointer or the object being pointed to that cannot be changed. The qualifier before the pointer modifier indicates the object being pointed to is `const`:

```
const char *p = buffer;   // pointer to const char
p = name;     // ok
*p = 'x';     // error!
```

The qualifier after the modifier indicates the pointer itself cannot be changed:

```
char * const p = buffer;  // const pointer to char
*p = 'X';         // ok
p = name;         // error!
```

The address of a `const` object cannot be assigned to a pointer to non-`const` because such an assignment could result in a change of the `const` through the pointer.

```
const char space = ' ';
const char *p = &space;   // ok
char *q = &space;       // error!
```

1.9 Exercises

Exercise 1-1. Write a C++ program that tells you how many bits are used to represent objects of type `char`, `short`, `int`, and `long`. □

Exercise 1-2. †Given the declarations

```
int &a = 12;
int *b;
int *&c = b;
int *d[5];
```

what are the types of the following expressions?

```
a
b
*b
```

```
c
*c
d[2]
*d
**d
c[-2]
c-2
*(c-2)
&c
```

□

Exercise 1-3. †Given the declarations

```
char c;
const char cc = 'a';
char *pc;
const char *pcc;
char *const cpc = &c;
const char *const cpcc = &cc;
char *const *pcpc;
```

which of the following assignments are legal, which are illegal, and why?

```
c = cc;
cc = c;
pcc = &c;
pcc = &cc;
pc = &c;
pc = &cc;
pc = pcc;
pc = cpc;
pc = cpcc;
cpc = pc;
*cpc = *pc;
pc = *pcpc;
**pcpc = *pc;
*pc = **pcpc;
```

□

Exercise 1-4. Give a verbal rendering of each of the following declarations:

```
int **a;
int *&b = 0;
int **&c = 0;
int * const d = 0;
int const *e;
int const *const *f;
int * const* *const g = 0;
int (*h)(int *);
int *(*j)();
int (*&k)() = 0;
int (*l);
int (*m)[12];
int (*n[12]);
int *o[12];
int (*p[12])();
int (**q[12])();
int (*(*r)[12])();
int *&(**(*s[3])[12])();
int (*t(int))(int *);
```

□

Exercise 1-5. Use typedefs to simplify the declarations of the previous exercise. □

Exercise 1-6. Describe the difference between the integer constant defined by the declaration

```
        const int i = 12;
```

and the integer literal 12. □

Exercise 1-7. Explain the semantics of each of the following functions:

```
    void
    swap1( int *a, int *b ) {
        int t = *a;
        *a = *b;
        *b = t;
    }
```

```
void
swap2( int &a, int &b ) {
    int t = a;
    a = b;
    b = t;
}

void
flop( int a, int b ) {
    int t = a;
    a = b;
    b = t;
}
```

□

Exercise 1-8. Devise a mechanism to force a compilation error if a given constant expression does not have a specified value. Of what use would such a technique be? □

Exercise 1-9. Show how a reference formal parameter can be used to supply detailed error information to the caller of a function. □

CHAPTER 2: **Procedural Programming**

A program is a sequence of operations on data structures that implements an algorithm or procedure to solve a problem. For most problems, the procedure is long and complicated enough that a program is difficult to implement and costly to maintain without methods for managing its size and complexity. Procedural programming techniques provide methods for dividing and structuring programs so that they are easy to build, understand, and maintain. These techniques focus on organizing the sequence of operations in the program and for the most part ignore the data structures on which the operations are performed.

In C++, a program starts execution with the `main` function, after the initialization of static data structures. Practically, `main` never contains all the operations in the program, for some are always delegated to other functions or built into the data structures using features that are presented in Chapter 3. In this chapter, we will use only simple forms of data structures and cover the use of procedural programming techniques in designing and organizing the functions in a C++ program.

2.1 Functions as Modules

A function is a module that encapsulates a sequence of operations. Functions have parameters so that their operations are generalized to apply to any actual arguments of the right type. The inputs to a function are the arguments and the global data objects that are used in the function. The results are its return value, modifications made through pointer and reference arguments, changes to global data, and effects external to the program.

The inputs and results are the interface to the function module. Users need only understand this interface to use the function. The actual sequence of operations that implements the function is a hidden detail, so the function can be considered a single abstract operation. Designing and implementing

33

the functions in a program can be thought of as building special operations that solve a given problem.

Programs must not only satisfy technical goals of correctly solving a problem but must also satisfy economic goals of being affordable. The modularity of functions can be used to make them more understandable and reusable, and, therefore, help reduce the cost of program implementation and maintenance.

Functions are easy to understand if they are designed to correspond to abstract operations needed in a solution. The function, and its use in the program, can then be thought of in terms of the problem, and not in the details of the implementation. For example, a function that takes as input an unsorted list and reorders the elements in ascending order may be described as the abstract operation "sort a list." The same abstract operation can be part of many problem solutions. The function that implements the operation can also be used in many programs if it is designed to be independent of its context in a particular program.

A function that does not use global data objects has only parameterized input. Instead of operating on a particular object given in the program, the function is an operation on any arguments of the correct type. The function can be reused with different inputs, not only in the original program, but also in other programs with the same type of data structures. The interface can be understood from its declaration, and the data object references in its implementation can be understood from declarations local to the function. With the parameterized input and locality of reference, the function is an easily reusable, somewhat self-documenting module.

2.2 Functional Decomposition

Functional decomposition is a method for subdividing a large program into functions. Starting with an overall description of what the program is to do, the method decomposes the action into a number of steps or abstract operations. Each step is implemented as a function in the program. Any function can itself be refined into substeps that can be implemented as functions. Finally, a level of detail is achieved when the steps can be implemented without further decomposition.

This design method results in a hierarchy of functions in which higher-level functions delegate work to lower-level functions. This method is also known as top-down design, because it starts at a high-level description of the program and then works through the refinement of the design to the low-level details of the implementation.

As an example, let us consider a program to sort a list of words. First we need to represent the list and the words in the program. The data structure for words are character strings, null-terminated sequences of characters accessed by pointers. The list is represented by an array containing pointers to the strings. This array has a maximum size and a size indicating how many strings have been entered into the array.

We give the `char *` string type a name using a `typedef` declaration, then set up the list and initialize it as empty.

```
typedef char *String;

const int max = 100;
String list[max];

int size = 0;
```

We are now ready to design the functions in our program. The problem is to take a list and produce a sorted list. At the highest level, this can be broken down into three operations:

```
read the original list
sort the list
print out the sorted list
```

We have three functions that are called from the `main` function in our program:

```
int input( String *, int );
void sort( String *, int );
void output( String *, int );

main() {
    size = input( list, max );
    sort( list, size );
    output( list, size );
}
```

Up to the maximum size of the list, `input` reads strings and enters them into the list, and returns the size of the list; `sort` puts the list elements in order; `output` prints out each string in the list. Notice that the array and size information have been made parameters of the functions. The functions are only used once in this program and could have accessed the global data directly instead of passing it as arguments. In this program, benefits of parameterized functions would come from easier maintenance and reuse of the functions in other programs.

The input, sort, and output functions are straightforward—except for reading and printing strings and the comparison of strings needed to do the sort. We delegate these tasks to lower-level functions and will not discuss them until later.

```
int readString( String & );
void printString( String );
int lessthan( String, String );

int
input( String *a, int limit ) {
    for( int i = 0; i < limit ; i++ )
        if( !readString( a[i] ) )
            break;
    return i;
}

void
output( String *a, int size ) {
    for( int i = 0; i < size; i++ )
        printString( a[i] );
}
```

```
void
sort( String *a, int n ) {
    // this uses a simple bubble sort algorithm
    int changed;
    do {
        changed = 0;
        for( int i = 0; i < n-1 ; i++ )
            if( lessthan( a[i+1], a[i] ) ) {
                String temp = a[i];
                a[i] = a[i+1];
                a[i+1] = temp;
                changed = 1;
            }
    } while( changed );
}
```

If it reads a string, readString returns 1 and 0 if it fails. The function lessthan returns 1 if the first argument is lexically less than the second, and 0 otherwise.

Finally, we come to the functions that do the exact work on the strings. The functions we need are already available in standard libraries.

```
#include <stdio.h>
#include <string.h>

int
readString( String &s ) {
    // read a string and copy it into
    // its own space, remembering to add
    // space for the terminating null

    const bufsize = 100;
    static char buffer[bufsize];
```

```
      if( scanf( "%s", buffer ) == EOF )
          return 0;
      s = new char[ strlen(buffer)+1 ];
      if( !s )  // new fails
          return 0;
      strcpy( s, buffer );
      return 1;
  }

  void
  printString( String s ) {
      printf(" %s", s );
  }

  int
  lessthan( String s1, String s2 ) {
      return strcmp( s1, s2 ) < 0;
  }
```

The function `readString` has a reference argument because it is meant to set the value of its argument to the newly created string. If a `String` instead of a `String &` argument type were used, the assignment to s would only set its local value without changing the value of the actual argument provided in the function call. The reference type lets the actual argument be set inside the function through the alias of the parameter name.

Note that `scanf` and `printf` do the string input and output and are declared in the standard library header file `stdio.h`. In addition, `scanf` returns a value EOF when it reaches the end of a file, and `strlen` gives the number of characters in a string, excluding the terminating null. Finally, `strcpy` copies one string to another; `strcmp` returns 0 if the strings have the same characters or returns a negative or positive value depending on whether the first argument comes lexically before or after the second. These functions are declared in `string.h`.

The top-down design of this program is represented by a hierarchical diagram:

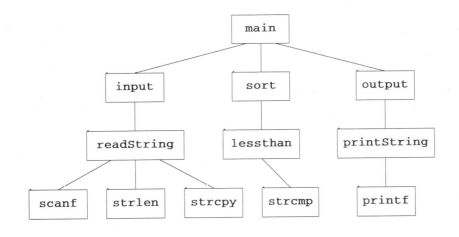

2.3 File Organization

The unit of compilation in C++ is the file. Any number of C++ files can be compiled and linked together to form an executable program. Declarations and definitions with *external linkage* allow cross-file reference of functions and data. The usual way of providing access to the external definitions in a file is to create a separate *header file* that contains the external declarations and supporting type definitions needed to use the functions and objects in the file correctly. The declarations in the header file are then included in any file that uses the external functions or objects. Functions and global objects declared as `static` have *internal linkage* and cannot be referenced outside the file in which they are declared. Global objects declared as `const` also have internal linkage unless explicitly declared `extern`.

Separating a large program into files can ease the process of developing, understanding, and maintaining a program. For example, a number of programmers can work on the same program simultaneously without interfering with one another; related functions and data structures can be grouped together to make them easy to read and understand; local modifications can be made with limited external effect.

Code separated out into a file is also easier to pick up for reuse in another program. This is the typical way code is reused, for example, in libraries. We have already shown the use of the standard input/output and string libraries. The functions declared in `stdio.h` and `string.h` are provided in publicly available files. The client code links to these libraries to form the complete program.

Since we designed the string-array functions in our example to be general, we will reorganize our list sort program and put the functions into a file that can be used in other programs.

We put the `main` function in a file called `main.cc`. A `.cc` at the end of a file name is the convention we use to indicate that it contains C++ program text. File naming conventions differ in various C++ programming environments. We make the file-scope data declarations `static` so access to the data from outside the file can only be done through pointers passed through function interfaces.

```
#include "strarray.h"

const int max = 100;
static String list[max];

static int size = 0;

main() {
    size = input( list, max );
    sort( list, size );
    output( list, size );
}
```

When `main.cc` is compiled, the contents of file `strarray.h` are inserted into the text at the `#include`. The definitions needed to use the following string-array functions are contained in `strarray.h`:

```
typedef char *String;

int input( String *, int );
void sort( String *, int );
void output( String *, int );
```

The definitions of the functions declared in `strarray.h` are put in `strarray.cc`. In rearranging our functions, we have also gotten rid of `printString` because it did not add anything to the operation already provided by `printf`.

```
#include <stdio.h>
#include <string.h>
#include "strarray.h"

static int
readString( String &s ) {
    // nothing new
}

static int
lessthan( String s1, String s2 ) {
    // nothing new
}

int
input( String *a, int limit ) {
    // nothing new
}

void
output( String *a, int size ) {
    for( int i = 0; i < size; i++ )
        printf( " %s", a[i] );
}

void
sort( String *a, int n ) {
    // nothing new
}
```

Notice that the auxiliary functions readString and lessthan have been declared static, indicating that they have internal linkage and cannot be accessed from other files. Since their use is restricted to this file, they can be changed, or even deleted, according to modifications needed by functions in this file without affecting external users.

Along with the standard headers that declare the library functions used in the implementation, strarray.cc includes its interface header strarray.h. This is done to get the needed type definition of String and as a consistency check between the declarations and implementations.

In order to call a C function from a C++ program, the C function must be declared to have C linkage.

```
extern "C" int printf( const char *, ... );
```

The `stdio` functions are part of the standard C library and are declared `extern "C"` in `stdio.h`. A number of functions can be declared to have C linkage with a bracketing linkage declaration:

```
extern "C" {
    int printf( const char *, ... );
    int scanf( const char *, ... );

    /* other C functions */

} /* end extern "C" */
```

Standard header files contain the proper linkage specifications for library functions, so C++ programmers typically do not need to deal with C linkage declarations unless they mix their own C and C++ files in a program.

2.4 Structured Programming

The use of structured programming techniques helps to make a function implementation understandable. The methods include using regular control structures, partitioning the function into blocks, formatting, and annotating the code with comments.

Control statements allow branches and loops to be implemented in such a way that the flow of control in a function can be followed easily. The statements give control structures regular, recognizable forms. C++ control statements are branches: `if`, `if-else`, `switch`; and loops: `for`, `while`, `do-while`. There are also a number of jump statements: `break`, for jumping out of loops and switches; `continue`, for progressing to the next loop iteration; `return`, for function return; and the infamous `goto`. Because of its generality in allowing jumps to anywhere in a function, a `goto` can make the sequence of operations in the function hard to follow and understand. Any use of a `goto` should be examined to see if it can be recoded using branch or loop statements.

Jumps can create problems not only because they obscure the flow of control. It is illegal for control to jump over a declaration with an initializer into the scope of that declaration, either with a `goto`:

```
    goto label;
    int i = 3;    // Error!
  label:
    i++;
```

or in a control structure:

```
  switch( x ) {
      int i = 0;    // Wrong!
  case 1: {
      int j = 1;    // Ok.
      break;
  }
  case 2:
      // etc.
  default:
      break;
  }
```

The only correct way to jump over a declaration with an initializer is to bypass the entire scope of the declaration.

All functions contain at least the block that is their body. The function parameter declarations are considered to be within that block. Blocks can be nested within other blocks.

Most often, blocks are used to group collections of statements within control structures. They can also be used to localize names that have limited use. For example, in the sort function, temp is declared within the block in which it is used.

```
      if( lessthan( a[i+1], a[i] ) ) {
          String temp = a[i];
          // etc.
      }
```

The local variable is initialized when the flow of control passes its point of declaration and goes out of existence when control leaves the block immediately enclosing the declaration. If temp were declared at an outer block, its purpose would not be so clearly understood from the context of its declaration, and there would be no useful initializing value available. Keeping the declaration at local block scope also allows the common, mnemonic name to be reused in other scopes.

Declarations are statements and can appear any place a statement can within a block. This flexibility allows names to be declared and initialized at the point of their first use. For example, the first clause in a `for` loop control can be a declaration-statement so a loop index can be declared there.

```
for( int i = 0; i < limit ; i++ )  {
   // etc.
}
return i;
```

The scope of a name extends from its point of declaration to the end of its block. Notice that, in this example, i is still available after the loop terminates. It goes out of scope at the end of the block that contains the `for` statement.

Formatting conventions are important for making a function readable. Most important for conveying the control structure of the function is the use of indentation to indicate the nesting of statements and blocks. Commonly sought sections of text should also be easy to find. For example, declarations, the beginning and end of function blocks, and labels should be clearly visible. Code sections can be highlighted by different indentation levels, surrounding white space, and position at the start of a line or the beginning of a block. Comments can also be used to mark sections of code.

There are two ways to separate comments from code in C++. Block comments start with /* and end with */; line comments start with // and go to the end of the line. Comments can be used to give overview explanations of functions or complicated sections of code. They can also explain statements with subtle or hidden implications. For example, hidden order dependencies between operations should be pointed out as well as assumptions on which the implementation is based.

```
/*
    The global variable flag1 must be set
    before the call to func1 because it sets
    the context for the later call to func2
*/


// Assumes ASCII Character Set
```

Comments also should be used in noting irregularities. For example, a comment like

```
// this is a kludge
```

points out an irregular bug fix in the program, although it is not very helpful. It is better to make the comment informative:

```
// ad hoc correction of roundoff error
```

Perhaps the most important way of commenting a function is to choose function and variable names that make their use self-explanatory. In particular, function names should convey the meaning of the abstract operation that the function implements, as in the above example with `input`, `sort`, and `output`. If meaningful and mnemonic names are used in a program, there is often only occasional need for additional comments. If meaningful names are not used, it is unlikely that any added comments will make the code easy to understand.

The previous discussion assumes that the programmer wants to help others understand his or her program. A program can be written to solve a problem without consideration for future use, or, in order to keep others from changing or reusing the program, it can be deliberately made to be obscure. The tactics of removing comments and formatting, as well as substituting names, are often used to make stealing code very costly for competitors. Other than for overt hostile acts, however, writing obscure code and leaving out comments are bad ideas. Most programs eventually require maintenance, whether or not they are maintainable. Programs that are difficult to understand are hard to update without causing damage with the change. The cost of maintenance will accumulate or the program will have to be discarded. To prolong the usefulness of their work, programmers should make their programs understandable.

2.5 Overloaded and Inline Functions

We have discussed how functions can be used as implementations of abstract operations and how function names document the operations. This use is further supported by the features of *overloaded* and *inline* functions.

Overloading allows the same name to be used for different function implementations, as long as the implementations can be distinguished by the type or number of their parameters. In this way the same abstract operation can be implemented on different types of operands without concocting artificial names to differentiate the functions.

For example, we can overload `sort` to work on two types of lists.

```
typedef char *String;

void sort( String *, int );
void sort( int *, int );
```

The first instance sorts an array of strings, the second sorts an array of integers. The function call

```
sort( list, size );
```

invokes the first instance if `list` has type `String *` or the second instance if it has type `int *`.

Inline functions support the use of small functions when, for reasons of efficiency, a programmer is reluctant to use a function call to invoke the few statements that implement an abstract operation. The specifier `inline` on a function declaration is a hint to the compiler to optimize a call to that function with an inline expansion of the function body. Inline expansion does not change the semantics of the function call. Any function but `main` may be declared inline but, depending on the capabilities of the compiler and the context of the call, the optimization of the function call may not always be accomplished. Like a function declared `static`, an inline function can be used only in the file in which it is defined because the definition must be visible at the point of call for the optimization to be possible. For an inline function to be used across files, it should be included in a header file.

Code that uses an inline function must be recompiled if the inline function changes in any way. Usually, the caller of a function need only be recompiled if the called function's interface changes. The cost of the performance improvements of inline optimization is the loss of modularity of compiled code.

In our example, the string comparison operator `lessthan` is a natural candidate for an inline function because it contains only a single statement.

```
inline int
lessthan( String s1, String s2 ) {
    return strcmp( s1, s2 ) < 0 ;
}
```

Below we use both function overloading and the inline `lessthan` in an extended version of our list-sort example. This example first sorts a list of strings, then a list of numbers. The lists are again implemented as arrays, but now there are two arrays with different types of elements.

```
#include "arrays.h"

const int max = 100;
static String strlist[max];
static int intlist[max];

static int size = 0;

main() {
    // Read, sort, and write a list of words
    size = input( strlist, max );
    sort( strlist, size );
    output( strlist, size );

    // Read, sort, and write a list of numbers
    size = input( intlist, max );
    sort( intlist, size );
    output( intlist, size );
}
```

The header file `arrays.h` contains the declarations of the overloaded array functions.

```
typedef char* String;

int input( String *, const int );
int input( int *, const int );

void output( String *, const int );
void output( int *, const int );

void sort( String *, const int );
void sort( int *, const int );
```

The functions are provided in `arrays.cc`. The full implementation of both versions of the overloaded functions is presented to show that they are almost duplicates. This demonstrates another kind of function reuse: reuse by stealing code and editing. Put another way, a generic function-text template was used for both functions, and simple text substitutions were used to make the necessary type differentiations.

```
#include <stdio.h>
#include <string.h>
#include "arrays.h"

static int
readString( String &s ) {
    // nothing new, see above
}

inline int
lessthan( String s1, String s2 ) {
    return strcmp( s1, s2 ) < 0 ;
}

int
input( String *a, const int limit ) {
    for( int i = 0; i < limit ; i++ )
        if( !readString( a[i] ) )
            break;
    return i;
}

int
input( int *a, const int limit ) {
    for( int i = 0; i < limit ; i++ )
        if( scanf( "%d", a+i ) == EOF )
            break;
    return i;
}

void
output( String *a, const int size ) {
    printf( "\nlist:" );
    for( int i = 0; i < size; i++ )
        printf( " %s", a[i] );
    printf("\n");
}
```

```
void
output( int *a, const int size ) {
    printf( "\nlist:" );
    for( int i = 0; i < size; i++ )
        printf( " %d", a[i] );
    printf( "\n" );
}

void
sort( String *a, const int n ) {
    int changed;
    do {
        changed = 0;
        for( int i = 0; i < n-1 ; i++ )
            if( lessthan( a[i+1], a[i] ) ) {
                String temp = a[i];
                a[i] = a[i+1];
                a[i+1] = temp;
                changed = 1;
            }
    } while( changed );
}

void
sort( int *a, const int n ) {
    int changed;
    do {
        changed = 0;
        for( int i = 0; i < n-1 ; i++ )
            if( a[i+1] < a[i] ) {
                int temp = a[i];
                a[i] = a[i+1];
                a[i+1] = temp;
                changed = 1;
            }
    } while( changed );
}
```

A warning needs to be given on the use of overloaded functions. Overloading conceptually unifies different functions in a program, but it does so by introducing ambiguity to the function name. In the overloaded sort example it is not too difficult to identify the function called by

```
sort( list, size );
```

Since there are no automatic conversions that result in the argument types, the type given by the declarations of list directly indicates which of the two functions is to be invoked. Given a multiply overloaded function name, and a number of conversions among possible argument types, however, the identification of the function can become complicated. The positive use of overloading to convey conceptual unity must be balanced with the negative results of having ambiguous names obscure what the program actually does.

2.6 Template Functions

The overloaded sort functions in the example above are almost identical implementations of the same algorithm. The text of the functions differ only where declarations or operations need to be made parameter-type specific. If the functions are overloaded for closely related types that support identical operations, they will differ only in their type declarations. C++ template functions allow users to declare a set of overloaded functions and provide one function definition for function instances of related types.

Below are the overloaded function declarations from arrays.h changed to template declarations.

```
template<class T> int input( T* a, int const limit );

template<class T> void output( T* a, const int size );

template<class T> void sort( T* a, const int n );
```

The <class T> is the template parameter list. In this context, the keyword class indicates that T is a type name, holding the place for the actual type in an instantiation of the template. These templates declare a set of potential overloaded function instances for input, output, and sort, including the instances for String and int. Given a template declaration, when one of these functions is called, overloaded function resolution may include the expansion of a template definition to create a function of a matching type.

To take advantage of the template declarations, we replace the int versions of the functions with template definitions that be instantiated with any numeric type.

```
template<class T> int
input( T* a, int const limit ) {
  double temp;
  for( int i = 0; i < limit ; i++ )
    if( scanf( "%lf", &temp ) == EOF )
       break;
    else {
       a[i] = (T)temp;
       if (a[i] != temp) {
          printf("error: input %f truncated\n",
              temp);
          a[i] = 0;
       }
    }
  return i;
}

template<class T> void
output( T *a, const int size ) {
   printf( "\nlist:" );
   for( int i = 0; i < size; i++ )
      printf( " %f", (double) a[i] );
   printf( "\n" );
}

template<class T> void
sort( T *a, const int n ) {
   int changed;
   do {
      changed = 0;
      for( int i = 0; i < n-1 ; i++ )
         if( a[i+1] < a[i] ) {
             T temp = a[i];
             a[i] = a[i+1];
             a[i+1] = temp;
             changed = 1;
         }
   } while( changed );
}
```

The above function definitions will work for any numeric type replacement
for T. Since the scanf and printf formatting statements are different for
each type, we do the input and output as double, a type that includes the

range of values from the other numeric types, and convert to and from the type stored in the array. Alternatively, we could have used overloaded read and write functions that work for all numeric types.

We can now use the templates to sort arrays of any numeric type.

```
#include "arrays.h"

const int max = 100;
static double dlist[max];
static short slist[max];
static String strlist[max];

static int size = 0;

main() {
    // Read, sort, and write a list of doubles
    size = input( dlist, max );
    sort( dlist, size );
    output( dlist, size );

    // Read, sort, and write a list of short ints
    size = input( slist, max );
    sort( slist, size );
    output( slist, size );

    // Read, sort, and write a list of Strings
    size = input( strlist, max );
    sort( strlist, size );
    output( strlist, size );

    return 0;
}
```

The function calls with dlist will match with the template resulting in the expansion of the template creating the functions

```
int input( double* a, int const limit );
void output( double* a, const int size );
void sort( double* a, const int n );
```

Likewise, the function calls with slist will result in the generation of the functions

```
int input( short* a, int const limit );
void output( short* a, const int size );
void sort( short* a, const int n );
```

The call `input( strlist, max )` does not match the template definition because conversions between `char*` and `double` are illegal. The calls with `strlist` will resolve to the old `String` versions of the overloaded functions.

A drawback to the use of templates is that implicit template expansion employed to resolve an overloaded function call occurs before the application of conversions to match arguments to parameter types. This may result in undesired template instantiation instead of reuse of an existing function instance with a converted argument. For example, given the template function declaration

```
template<class T> void f(T);
```

and the two calls

```
int i;
short s;

f(i);
f(s);
```

two instances of f are generated: `f(int)` and `f(short)`. If a template is not used, a single function instance declared

```
void f(int);
```

accommodates both function calls, with the argument s being automatically converted to match the `int` parameter type.

Template functions are primarily useful in conjunction with generic class types, discussed in Chapter 4.

2.7 Arguments and Return Values

A function type consists of both its parameter types and its return type. In a call, the function to be called is first identified by its name. Then the identification is verified by whether the arguments in the call match the declared parameter types or can be made to match through available conversions. The choice among overloaded function instances is made by matching argument types to parameter types.

Functions that take arbitrary numbers and types of arguments have their types specified with a trailing ellipsis in the parameter list.

```
void error( const char *, ... );
```

This declaration declares `error` to be a function returning no value, taking a string first argument and any number and type of additional arguments. The `const` indicates that the string cannot be changed through the pointer, so string literals can be safely used in a call. Presumably, the first argument in a call to `error` will contain the information needed to interpret later arguments.

Arguments are automatically converted to the parameter types in a function call. If the conversion is to a class type parameter, a predefined conversion might first be applied to match the argument to the type needed by the user-defined class constructor, as was shown in the `class complex` example in Chapter 1. If the conversion is from a class type argument to a non-class parameter type, an additional predefined conversion might be applied after the user-defined one. For arguments that match an ellipsis parameter specification, small integral types are converted to `int` or `unsigned`, and floating point types are converted to `double`. Otherwise no argument conversions are applied.

When a function is executed, the formal parameters in a function definition are initialized with the actual arguments of the function call. When a value is returned from a function, it is used to initialize the result. The fact that arguments and return values are initialized, rather than assigned, is especially important for `const` and reference types as well as for class types with constructors, where initialization is significantly different from assignment.

The formal parameters of a function are local variables within the function block. After being initialized by a function call, they can be used like any other variable, including being assigned to and having their value changed. A `const` specifier means that the declared object *cannot* have its value changed after initialization. A `const` parameter will not be altered from the original value passed as an argument. Such a parameter declaration can prevent erroneous changes to what should be fixed values. For example, in our list sort, the size of the list to be sorted is fixed. To indicate this, the parameter could have been declared `const`.

```
sort( String *, const int );
```

Except for reference parameters, formal parameters are different objects from the actual arguments. Once they are initialized with the values of the arguments, they can be used and assigned locally without any effect external to the function. As discussed in Chapter 1, reference parameters are *not* separate objects from the actual arguments. Their initialization establishes the reference name as an alias for the object that is the initializer. Reference type parameters allow "call by reference," in which an assignment to the parameter inside the function results in a change of the value of the actual argument. A reference type was used for a parameter of `readString` because the string was returned through the argument.

```
int readString( String & );
```

A convenience feature in C++ that allows flexibility in the use of functions is *default argument initializers*. Default argument values can be given in a function declaration and are automatically supplied to function calls that have fewer than the declared number of arguments. For example, a function declared with three arguments, two with default initializers,

```
int
error( const char *msg, int level = 0, int kill = 0 );
```

can be called with one, two, or three arguments:

```
error( "you goofed" );
    // actual call: error( "you goofed", 0, 0 );
error( "you screwed up", 1 );
    // actual call: error( "you screwed up", 1, 0 );
error( "you blew it!", 3, 1 );
    // no default arguments used
```

Default arguments are particularly useful in minimizing the effects of changes to a program during maintenance. An existing function can be changed by adding arguments without having to alter source code for existing function calls. A declaration with a default argument initializer for the new parameter will allow the old calls to exist as before. This makes it easier to extend the behavior of a function.

As an example, we will change our string-array sort function to sort the list in either alphabetical order or reverse. First, in our header file, we add an argument type and default initializer to the function declaration.

```
void sort( String *, int, int descending = 0 );
```

The dummy argument name in the function declaration is not needed, except
as a comment to give the reader a clue about why the argument is there.
When files using the header are recompiled, a third argument of 0 will be automatically added to all calls of the string-array sort function, that have only
two arguments.

Now we adapt the sort function to use the new third argument. First, we
add a `greaterthan` function that compares two strings. Then `sort` is
changed to use a pointer-to-function variable to call either `lessthan` or
`greaterthan`. The inline specifier has no optimizing effect here because
the function call is through a pointer.

```
inline int
lessthan( String s1, String s2 ) {
    return strcmp( s1, s2 ) < 0 ;
}

inline int
greaterthan( String s1, String s2 ) {
    return strcmp( s1, s2 ) > 0 ;
}

void
sort( String *a, int n, int descending ) {

    int changed;
    typedef int (* Fptype)( String, String );

    // declare and initialize pointer to comparison function
    Fptype compare = descending ?
            &greaterthan : &lessthan;
```

```
    do {
        changed = 0;
        for( int i = 0; i < n-1 ; i++ )
            if( compare( a[i+1], a[i] ) ) {
                String temp = a[i];
                a[i] = a[i+1];
                a[i+1] = temp;
                changed = 1;
            }
    } while( changed );
}
```

The ? : operator that is used to select the comparison function is a conditional expression. If the first operand `descending` has a nonzero value, the second operand `&greaterthan` is evaluated and is the result of the expression. If `descending` is zero, the third operand `&lessthan` is evaluated and is the result of the expression.

The string-array function has been extended without affecting existing usage of the function except for the required recompilation of the files that include the changed header. New calls to `sort` can take advantage of its new functionality by setting its third argument.

```
#include "arrays.h"

const int max = 100;
static String strlist[max];

static int size = 0;
const int descending = 1;

main() {
    // Same as before
    size = input( strlist, max );
    sort( strlist, size );
    output( strlist, size );

    // Now, into descending order
    size = input( strlist, max );
    sort( strlist, size, descending );
    output( strlist, size );
}
```

2.8 Exercises

Exercise 2-1. Modify the string-sort program to be able to handle an arbitrary number of strings. Do not change the number or hierarchical relationships of the functions in your solution from that of the original solution. Is this a different solution to the problem or merely another version of the same solution? □

Exercise 2-2. Find another decomposition that solves the string-sort problem corresponding to the following conceptualization:

```
while read a string
    insert the string in sorted position
print the strings
```

Which solution is more efficient? Which solution is more easily adapted to interactive use? Which solution is better? □

Exercise 2-3. Often certain functions may be generally useful to other functions in a program. For example, an `error` function may be used whenever an error message is to be output, or a `lookup` function may used by any function needing to access stored information. How does the functional decomposition method, which produces a hierarchical design, hinder the identification of general utility functions? □

Exercise 2-4. †A token is a word or other significant group of characters in a text that is surrounded by separator characters like space, tab, or newline. Write a function that returns the address of the next token in its argument string while modifying the value of its argument to point one character past the end of the token. Include an optional second argument to the function that specifies what characters are considered to separate tokens. Use the function to write a version of `strlen`, a function that returns the length of its argument string. □

Exercise 2-5. Write a function,

```
int bsearch( int *array, int key, int num );
```

that performs a binary search for an integer key in a sorted array of integers. Rewrite `bsearch` to work with a) an array of `doubles` with a `double` key, b) an array of structures with an `int` key, c) an array of structures with a character string key, d) an array of pointers to structures with an `int` key, and e) an array of structures on disk, too large to read into memory in its entirety, with an `int` key. □

Exercise 2-6. Consider the following program:

```
void f( int ) {}
void f( long ) {}

main() {
    f( 40000 );
}
```

Which overloaded instance of `f` is invoked by your C++ compiler? Explain why this C++ program will exhibit different, correct behavior when compiled by different C++ compilers. □

Exercise 2-7. Discuss the pros and cons of the following `swap` function template.

```
template <class T>
void
swap( T &a, T &b ) {
    a ^= b;
    b ^= a;
    a ^= b;
}
```

□

CHAPTER 3: **Classes**

Functions and the data structures on which they operate are interdependent. Functions are designed to operate on particular data structures that, in turn, must be left in a correct state by the functions that use them. In the string-sort example in Chapter 2, the functions depend on the data structure that represents a string to be a null-terminated character array. If one of the functions erroneously overwrote the terminating null, other functions would not work correctly on the corrupted data structure. If the representation of the string were changed to a structure containing explicit length information instead of a terminating character, a new set of functions would have to be written to work on this new data structure. Dependencies among many functions and complicated data structures can be difficult to manage in large programs.

In C++, classes support a variety of ways of organizing programs and controlling dependencies among data structures and functions. Programming techniques using classes will be the subject of most of the rest of this book. To lay the groundwork for later discussion, this chapter introduces the features of C++ classes.

3.1 Class Types

Classes are user-defined aggregate data types. They may contain both data members representing the type and function members that implement operations on the type. Parts of the class can either be hidden or made explicitly available by use of `private` and `public` sections of the class. Members in `private` sections can be accessed only by member functions of that class or by other functions declared to be `friends` of the class. By using this information-hiding mechanism, a class can encapsulate a data structure so that only functions specified by the class can use it.

Here we reimplement the string-sort example using a class `String` type to represent strings. The class tag `String` is a type name for the class and can be used in the same way as a `typedef` name.

```
#include <stdio.h>
#include <string.h>

class String {
    char *str;
  public:
    String() { str = new char[1]; *str = '\0'; }
    String( const char * );
    void print() { printf( " %s", str ); }
    friend int operator <( const String &s1,
                const String &s2 )
        { return strcmp( s1.str, s2.str ) < 0; }
};
```

The underlying data structure used to represent a string has not changed: it is still a pointer to a null-terminated array of characters. Now, however, this structure is hidden as the member `str` in the private section of `String`. Only the `String` constructors, the member function `print`, and the friend function `operator` `<` can access the string representation. All the member functions are declared in the public section of the class and so are generally available for use.

The first two member functions have the same name as the class, which identifies them as *constructors* for the class. Whenever a `String` is created, a constructor is used to initialize it. The first `String` constructor takes no arguments and initializes `str` to point to an empty string. Operator `new` is used to allocate space to store the string. Since this function is short, its body is defined inside the class definition. This is a shorthand way of making a member or friend function `inline`.

The second constructor is only declared inside the class, so its definition must be provided elsewhere.

```
String::String( const char *s ) {
    if (s) {
        str = new char[ strlen(s)+1 ];
        strcpy( str, s );
    } else {
        // create a null string
        str = new char[1];
        *str = '\0';
    }
}
```

In a member function definition outside of the class, the function name must be qualified to indicate that the function referred to is within the scope of the class. Here, the scope qualifier `String::` indicates that this is the definition of a `String` member.

Member functions are always within the scope of their class. Therfore, the members of the class object on which a member function is operating can be referred to without a member access operator. Note that `String` and `print` refer to `str` without qualification. By contrast, the friend function

```
friend int operator < ( const String &s1,
                const String &s2 )
    { return strcmp( s1.str, s2.str ) < 0; }
```

must use the member access operator . to access the `str` member of its `String` arguments. Friend status makes the private member `str` accessible without error, but the function remains at the same scope it would be if it were not a friend.

Operator functions are a way of overloading the language-defined operators to apply to class type operands. Here the less than operator has been defined to compare two `String` reference arguments. The infix operator < can now be used to compare two `String` operands.

Completing the string-sort example, we can see how the `String` type can be used.

```
void
input( String *a, int limit, int &i ) {
    char buffer[100];
    for( i = 0; i < limit; i++ )
        if( scanf( "%s", buffer ) == EOF )
            break;
        else
            a[i] = String( buffer );
}
```

The function input reads strings into a list. The statement

```
a[i] = String( buffer );
```

forces a conversion that invokes a constructor to create a class String object from the characters in the input buffer. This String object is then assigned to a slot in the list array.

In the procedure that outputs the list, the String output function print is called for every element in the list using the . member access operator.

```
void
output( String *a, int size ) {
    printf( "\nlist: " );
    for( int i = 0; i < size; i++ )
        a[i].print();
    printf( "\n" );
}
```

In the function that sorts the list, operator < is invoked using infix notation to compare elements in the list making this procedure look exactly like the sort on the numeric list in Chapter 2, except for the types of the list elements.

```
void
sort( String *a, int n ) {
    int changed;
    do {
        changed = 0;
        for( int i = 0; i < n-1; i++ )
            if( a[i+1] < a[i] ) {
                String temp = a[i];
                a[i] = a[i+1];
                a[i+1] = temp;
                changed = 1;
            }
    } while( changed );
}
```

Finally, the main function reads, sorts, and outputs the list.

```
const int max = 10;
static String list[max];

static int size = 0;

main() {
    input( list, max, size );
    sort( list, size );
    output( list, size );
}
```

This looks exactly the same as the version in Chapter 2 that used a char
* implementation of type String. There is a difference, however. In this
case, the constructor with no arguments is called to initialize each element of
list. The list array starts off with each element representing a proper
String instead of being initialized to zeros. Although it doesn't matter for
this program, automatic initialization of class objects through constructors
makes program correctness more likely because the data structures encapsulated in the object automatically start off in a correct state.

3.2   Data Members

The definition of a class type, like that of String in the previous section, serves as a pattern for objects of the class type. When a class type object is created, space is allocated for the object and instances of the data

members are created and initialized as components of the object. Like other data objects in C++, objects of class type can be created in different scopes and exist for different durations. File scope objects are created before the start of the program execution and exist until the program ends. Local `static` objects are initialized before they are used and, if created, endure until the program ends. Parameters and local objects are created when program execution reaches the point of their declaration and remain in existence until the block in which they are declared is exited. Objects created dynamically using operator `new` exist until they are explicitly destroyed using operator `delete`. Temporary objects are also created to hold intermediate results of expression evaluation and function return values.

Component members of a class object can be accessed with the member access operators `.` and `->`. The `.` operator is used with class objects.

```
String s;
s.str;
```

The `->` operator is used with pointers to class objects.

```
String *sp = new String;
sp->str;
```

The `new` operator creates an object of the type specified by its argument and returns a pointer to the new object.

Class data member types can be of any of the language-defined types, a previously defined class type, a pointer to a class type, or a reference to a class type. Pointers or references to a class type do not need to have that class defined but only need to have the class name declared. For example:

```
class Node;  // declare the name only
Node *np; // use it to declare a pointer
```

By using a pointer or a reference to the class type as a member of the class, it is possible to build recursive class structures. For example, a binary tree node would contain pointers to its left and right children.

```
class Node {
    Node *left, *right;
    // etc.
};
```

Note that these have to be pointers or references; a `Node` cannot contain a `Node` directly.

Each data member instance in a class object is allocated the amount of space needed to represent its type. There may be padding between members of a class object, depending on the alignment needs of different machines, and the compiler may add implicit data members to implement features described in later chapters.

One way of saving space in a class object is to use the same space for more than one member. There is a type of class in which data members are not allocated sequentially, but overlap, all starting at the initial location in the object. This kind of class is called a `union`. The `union` specifier replaces `class` in a declaration of a union type. Members of a union type are `public` by default.

```
union Un_type {
    int i;
    double d;
    char *p;
};
```

When a union type object is instantiated, its size and alignment is adjusted so that all the members occupy the same location in the object. The union members can be referenced using the usual member access operators. The result of accessing a union member is that the single location is interpreted according to the member type.

```
Un_type u;

u.i = 1;  // int value stored in u
u.d = 3.1415;    // double value overwrites int value

char c = *u.p;   // danger! probably bad pointer value
```

There is some peril in storing union members as one type and accessing them as another. A legal value for one member need not be legal for a different member. For correct uses of unions, there usually needs to be information available to indicate which member to use. Unions can be made members of classes when other members provide information on how to interpret the union member.

```
enum TypeCode{ is_int, is_double, is_charstar };

class Node {
  public:
    Node *left, *right;
    TypeCode code;
    Un_type info;
};
Node anode, *np = &anode;
```

In the example, the `code` in a `Node` object will indicate how to interpret the union member

```
int i = 0; double d = 0; char *p = 0;

switch( np->code ) {
    case is_charstar:
        p = np->info.p;
        break;
    case is_double:
        d = np->info.d;
        break;
    case is_int:
        i = np->info.i;
        break;
}
```

Since a `Node` contains only one type of information at a time, using a union to overlap the different type members saves space in a `Node` object.

Class members can be made to overlap in a similar way without the added notation of an explicit union member access by nesting an *anonymous union* in a class. An anonymous union has no tag and declares no member name.

```
class Node {
  public:
    Node *left, *right;
    TypeCode code;
    union {
        int i;
        double d;
        char *p;
    };
};
```

Here, i, d, and p are still allocated to overlap, but they can be accessed directly as members of Node.

```
int i = 0; double d = 0; char *p = 0;

switch( np->code ) {
    case is_charstar:
        p = np->p;
        break;
    case is_double:
        d = np->d;
        break;
    case is_int:
        i = np->i;
        break;
}
```

The use of unions is relatively rare in C++, as the use of inheritance with virtual functions, described in Chapter 5, provides a safer and more convenient alternative in many cases.

Another way to save space in a class object is to subdivide an integer-sized segment into a number of integer type data members each using a specific number of bits. *Bitfields* allow some control over space used in a class object when it is known that certain integral members will only take a small range of values. A bitfield may be specified by following the declaration of a data member with a colon and the size of the field.

```
class Node {
  public:
    Node *left, *right;
    unsigned int code: 2;
    unsigned int is_leaf: 1;
    unsigned int is_free: 1;
    //...
};
```

In the example above, code is allocated two bits in a Node object and can take on four values. The members is_leaf and is_free each have one bit and serve as two-valued flags. The fields are grouped together so that they are packed in the same segment of the object.

A programmer may be able to control the size of a class with bitfields and by grouping members to pack the space used in objects. The benefits of this control are implementation dependent. A programmer must be familiar with the sizes and alignments of types on the target machine, and with the behavior of the C++ compiler, in order to use this control successfully to save space in class objects.

Type declarations can be nested within a class. Nesting allows other classes, type definitions, and enum tags and symbolic values to be defined within the scope of a class. Using a nested declaration, the enum TypeCode can be made part of class Node. The nested enum values can be accessed as members of the class or by using the scope access operator ::.

```
class Node {
  public:
    Node *left, *right;
    enum TypeCode{ is_int, is_double, is_charstar };
    TypeCode code;
    union {
        int i;
        double d;
        char *p;
    };
} *np;
```

In this example, enumerator names are local to the class. They do not conflict with names in other scopes, and access to them could be restricted by putting them in the private section. Since the enum values are independent of any individual Node object, they should generally be referenced using the scope access operator :: instead of the . or -> member access operators.

```
switch( np->code ) {
    case Node::is_charstar:
        p = np->p;
        break;
    case Node::is_double:
        d = np->d;
        break;
    case Node::is_int:
        i = np->i;
        break;
}
```

Likewise, in declarations outside of the class, the nested enum type name is indicated with a scope specification.

```
Node::TypeCode code  = np->code;
```

Generally, data members are made `private` in a class. It is preferable to keep the data members accessible only to a small set of functions with special privileges. This restricts dependencies on data structure implementation and increases modularity of a program. Access protection is discussed later in this chapter. Hidden data is the basic feature on which the benefits of data abstraction are built. Data abstraction is the topic of Chapter 4.

3.3 Function Members

A function declared within a class definition and not specified as `friend` is a member function of that class. A member function can be defined within its class, in which case it is implicitly `inline`. The member access operators `.` and `->` are used in member function calls. The `.` operator is used with class objects.

```
String s;
s.print();
```

The `->` operator is used with pointers to class objects.

```
String *sp = new String;
sp->print();
```

As with nonmember functions, there is compile time checking of member function calls. The type of the class object is used to identify the function and the actual arguments are matched to the parameter types in the function declaration.

Member functions operate on the class type object with which they are called. A pointer to this object is a hidden argument in member functions and can be explicitly referred to in the function definition as `this`. No explicit use of `this` is needed to access a class member within a member function, as `this` is implicitly used for member references.

```
class String {
    char *str;
  public:
    //...
    void print() { printf( " %s", str ); }
    //...
};
```

In the above, `print` has an implicit argument `String *const this`. The reference to the member `str` in `print` is the same as `this->str`. When `print` is called, `this` is set to the address of the object used in the call. For example, `s.print()` sets `this` to the address of `s` and, therefore, within `print`, the `str` referred to is `(&s)->str` or `s.str`. In the call `sp->print()`, `this` is set to `sp` and the member access is to `sp->str`.

A pointer-to-constant cannot be passed as an argument declared as a regular pointer because the `const` object could be altered through unrestricted pointer access from within the function call. This restriction applies to the implicit `this` argument of member functions.

```
const String version("Release 4.0.1");

//...
version.print();// error! print called for const
```

The address of `version` in the above example has type `const String *const` which is a type mismatch to the `String *const this` argument of `print`. Since `print` in fact does not alter the object it works on, its declaration can be changed so that it can be applied to a `const String`.

```
class String {
    char *str;
  public:
    //...
    void print() const;
    //...
};
```

Adding `const` to a member function declaration after the argument list changes the type of the `this` argument to pointer-to-constant. Now `print` has an argument `const String *const this` and can be applied to a const String.

Each member function is logically nested within the scope of its class. If a member function definition is given outside the body of a class definition, the scope of the function must be indicated by the scope operator with the class name.

```
class X {
    int f();
};


int X::f() { /* etc. */ }
```

The nesting of member functions within class scope makes the scoping rules different for member functions than for nonmember functions. In a member function, the declaration of an identifier is sought first at block scope, then at class scope, and finally at file scope. It is, therefore, possible for a member declaration to hide a file scope declaration. In the following example, the identifier x in function X::f() refers to the member, not to the file scope variable x.

```
class X {
    int x;
    int f();
};

int x;

int X::f() { return x; }  // returns this->x
```

To reference the declaration of a file scope identifier hidden by a local or class scope declaration, the scope operator can be used. To change the above example so that X::f() returns the value of the file scope variable instead of the member, use :: to indicate the file scope x.

```
int X::f() { return ::x; }   // returns file scope x
```

The class scope is like a block around the member function. A declaration within a block scope of the function can hide the member declaration just as an inner block declaration can hide an outer block declaration. In the following case, X::f() returns the value of the local variable.

```
int X::f() { int x = 3; return x; }
```

Using the scope operator, the above can be changed to return either the member X::x or file scope variable ::x.

3.4 Operator Functions

Language-defined operators can be overloaded to work on class type operands. This is done by providing an operator function that takes at least one class or reference-to-class type argument. Operator function declarations and definitions are syntactically the same form as those of other functions except that the function name has the form operator # where # is the operator symbol being overloaded. The user-defined operators can be invoked with the usual infix expression syntax for the symbol # as well as with a function call using the function name operator #. The operands of the expression serve as the arguments to the function call.

Since they are invoked with the same syntax, operator functions must have the same number of operands as the language-defined versions of the operators. Overloaded operators have the same precedence as the corresponding built-in operators. Relationships among predefined operators, however, such as the equivalence of a+=b and a=a+b, or a[b] and *(a+b), or (&p)->x and p.x, do not hold for user-defined operators unless operator functions are implemented for both operations to make it so. The results of operator functions need not have any relation to the results of the predefined versions.

Suppose we add more operators to class complex of Chapter 1.

```
class complex {
    // etc.
    complex operator ++();     // prefix ++
    complex operator +=( complex );
};
```

The version of complex ++ declared here is the prefix form of the operator. An artificial extra int argument in either operator ++ or –– declarations indicate a postfix version.

```
complex operator ++(int); // postfix ++
```

The artificial argument serves only to differentiate the postfix operator from the prefix operator. The compiler provides a dummy value for this argument when the postfix operator is used.

The user-defined operator += may or may not be defined so that

```
c1 += c2;
```

is equivalent to

```
c1 = c1 + c2;
```

though it would be confusing if it were not. Since class complex is intended to act as a numeric type, it is better to implement += to behave analogously to the built-in arithmetic operators.

Operator functions can be non-member or member functions, with the exception of operators =, (), [] and -> which can only be member functions. If the operator function is a member, the implicit argument this is the first operand. In class String the operator <, which is implemented as a friend,

```
class String {
    char *str;
  public:
    friend int operator < ( const String &s1,
               const String &s2 )
       { return strcmp( s1.str, s2.str ) < 0; }
    // etc.
};
```

could also have been implemented as a member.

```
class String {
    char *str;
  public:
    int operator < ( const String &s2 ) const
       { return strcmp( str, s2.str ) < 0; }
    // etc.
};
```

If an operator function is a member, its first operand must always match the class type without conversions being applied. Operator functions are often intended to behave analogously to their language-defined versions, in which conversions are applied to either operand. For this reason, operator functions are often implemented as friend functions.

Operator functions are functions with odd names that work on class type arguments. They do not have to be called using infix notation, but can be

called in the same way as any other function. For a nonmember function, all
arguments are passed in the argument list.

```
class String {
    friend int operator < ( const String &,
                    const String &);
    // etc.
};

void sort( String *a, int n ) {
    // etc.
    if( operator < ( a[i+1], a[i] )) {
        // etc.
```

For member functions, a member access operator is used.

```
class String {
    int operator < ( const String &);
    // etc.
};

void sort( String *a, int n ) {
    // etc.
    if( a[i+1].operator <( a[i] ) ) {
        // and so on
```

Operator functions can make code obscure by disguising function calls
and should be used sparingly. They are best used to express concisely
functions that are exactly analogous to the built-in versions of the operators.
To repeat: operator functions are a purely syntactic convenience meant to
clarify, not obscure, code.

3.5 Static Members

Data or function class members declared `static` are independent of object instances. A static data member is created when the class is defined and
exists before there are any class objects. Both static data and functions can
be referenced without a class type object using the scope access operator `::`.
Since static members are independent of any particular class object, they can
have their addresses taken and have pointers set to them like any other object
or function with static storage duration.

As an example of static members, let's suppose we wanted to keep track of how many instances of `class String` have been created. To keep count, a static data member of `String` is incremented by each constructor. A static member function is also provided to utilize the information in the static data.

```
class String {
    char *str;
    static int count;
  public:
    String() { count++; str = new char; *str = 0; }
    String( char *s ) {
        count++;
        str = new char[ strlen(s)+1 ];
        strcpy( str, s );
    }
    static void usagereport();
    // etc.
}
```

The single instance of the static member `count` is initialized outside the `String` class body with a definition similar to one for global data, except for the class-scoped name:

```
int String::count = 0;
```

`String::count` is incremented for each `String` object initialized with a constructor. To find out how many `String` type objects have been created at any point in the program, a function with the proper access permission can reference `String::count`, or a call can be made to the static function to print the information.

```
void String::usagereport() {
    printf( "Report on String Usage:" );
    printf( " %d Strings created\n", count );
}
```

The static member function call can be made without a `String` instance using the scope operator instead of a member access operator.

```
String::usagereport();
```

Unlike other member functions that operate on a particular instance of a class object, a static member function does not have an implicit `this` argument. The static function `usagereport` can access the static data `count`; however, it has no `this` pointer to a `String` argument through which to access the per-instance data `str`. Like other member functions, `usagereport` is within the scope of the class and does not need a scope operator to access static members.

3.6 Access Protection and Friends

Class members can be `public` (generally accessible) or `private` (access restricted to member and friend functions). The accessibility of members is indicated by their declaration in a section of the class definition headed by the label `public` or `private`. These labels can appear any number of times in a class definition and in any order. The first section of a class definition begins as private until a label indicates a different protection level.

There is a third protection level in C++ that comes into play when class inheritance is used. A member can be specified as `protected` in the same way that it can be specified `public` or `private`. When inheritance is not being used, protected members have the same access restrictions as private members. The use of inheritance and protected members is discussed in Chapter 5.

Functions that have been declared `friend` in a class definition are not members of the class but have permission to access the private members of objects of the class type. One class can also be declared `friend` of another class, indicating that all member functions of the friend class are friends.

```
class X {
    friend class Y;
    int i;
    void f();
};

class Y {
    int f1( X& );
    void f2( X& );
    // etc.
};
```

In this example, the private members of X type objects, like the members `i` and `f()` of the X& arguments, can be accessed inside `Y::f1` and `Y::f2`.

The member access operators . or -> must be used by friend functions because only members have this.

We have already noted that, in a union, members are public unless otherwise indicated. *Structures* are another type of class. They are the same as classes except for the default member access level. In a structure definition, struct replaces class in the type definition. The first section of a structure begins as public until a label indicates a different protection level.

```
struct String {
    String();
    String( const char * );
    void print();
    friend int operator < ( const String &s1,
                const String &s2 );
    // etc.
  private:
    char *str;
};
```

In the above version of String, the member functions are all public, whereas the data member str is private.

C++ access control helps to prevents unauthorized use of private class members, but it does not necessarily isolate users of the public interface from the private part of the class. For example, addition of a private member can change the layout of a class object so that code accessing public members needs to be recompiled. The public part of a class is the accessible part of the class implementation, it is not the declaration of an interface that is separated from the implementation.

3.7 Initialization and Conversions

If a class has constructors, a constructor always is used to initialize objects of the class type when they are created. In the string-sort example in this chapter, the constructor taking no arguments initializes the String array. Constructor arguments can be given to initialize objects at the point of declaration.

```
String s1( "hi" );

String s2 = "hi";
```

In the declarations above, both forms of initializers are used as constructor arguments to initialize the `String` objects `s1` and `s2`.

Constructor arguments can also be given when objects are created with operator `new`.

```
String *sp;
sp = new String( "hello" );
```

In the above, `sp` is set to point at a `String` that was initialized with a constructor using the argument `"hello"`. If arguments are not provided when a class object is declared or created, a constructor taking no arguments or having default arguments is used.

Class objects that are members of other class objects are also initialized with a constructor. Arguments for the constructor can be given in the member initialization list of the constructor of the enclosing class. Initializing values for any member, not only constructor arguments, can be specified with a member initializer. Members that require initialization, like constant or reference type members, must have their initializers so specified. The member initialization list is separated by a colon from the constructor's argument list in the constructor's definition. It contains a list of member names, each of which is followed by a parenthesized list of constructor arguments or an initializing value.

```
class Node {
    Node *left, *right;
    const int code;
    String str;
  public:
    Node( int, char * );
    void print() { str.print(); }
    // etc.
};

Node::Node( int c, char *s )
    : code( c ), str( s ) { }
```

The `Node` constructor in the above example initializes the member `code` with the value of the argument `c` and passes its second argument `s` to the `String` constructor to initialize the `Node` member `str`. Given the above definition of `Node`, the code fragment

```
Node *np = new Node( acode, "hello" );
np->print();
```

prints out

```
hello
```

It might seem that the use of the member initialization list could be replaced by assignments in the body of the constructor.

```
Node::Node( int c, char *s ) {
    code = c; // error! assignment to const.
    str = s;
}
```

For most non-class data members, there is not much difference between an initialization and a first assignment. A `const` member, however, must be set by initialization since its value cannot be changed by assignment. Similarly, a reference member must be initialized. The integer member `code` is a `const` and, therefore, must have its value set by an initializer, not by an assignment in the constructor.

The member `str` can be set by assignment in the `Node` constructor, but this will cause it to be set twice: once by initialization and once by assignment. The `String` class type has constructors:

```
class String {
    char *str;
  public:
    String();
    String( const char *s );
    // etc.
};
```

Whenever a `String` object is created, it is *always* initialized. Since no other initializer is specified, the default `String` constructor is used to initialize `str` when it is created. The assignment within the body of the `Node` constructor replaces the initial value of `str` with one that is the result of the conversion of the right-hand side of the assignment. There have been two calls to `String` constructors: one to initialize `str` and the second to convert `s` before the assignment. Assignment is not the same as initialization. Arguments for constructors that initialize members must be indicated in the member initializer list along with the initializers for `const` and reference type members.

A constructor creates a class object from its arguments and so converts the arguments to the class type. Constructors are not only initializers but conversion operators. This was shown in the string-sort program in which a pointer to an array of characters was converted to a `String`, using a function-call style conversion, and assigned to an element of a `String` array.

```
a[i] = String( buffer );
```

When a constructor takes one argument, it can also be invoked using the cast form of conversion operation

```
a[i] = ( String )buffer;
```

Function-call style or cast style conversions are generally interchangeable, although multiple-argument constructor conversions require the function-call style, and syntactically complex conversion type specifications require the cast style:

```
x = X(i,j);        // convert i and j to an X
fp = (int (*)())g; // convert g to a function pointer
```

A type definition can be used to simplify the expression of a type to allow a function-call style cast:

```
typedef int (*Fp)();
fp = Fp(g);
```

Expression operands and function call arguments are automatically converted to the correct type if the required combination of language- and user-defined conversion operations is available. It is an error if the choice of available conversions is ambiguous. An explicit conversion operation is necessary to force a conversion that cannot be done automatically.

Since conversions are applied implicitly, an explicit conversion operation is not needed to convert the `const char *` input buffer to a `String` in the string-sort example. The availability of the `String( const char * )` constructor provides a user-defined conversion from the right-hand-side to the left-hand-side type. An assignment that takes advantage of the automatically applied conversion

```
a[i] = buffer;
```

works just as well as the assignment with explicit conversion. In either case, the `String` constructor is used to convert the right-hand side.

   Constructors provide conversions *to* the class type. It is also possible to provide conversions *from* the class type with conversion operator functions. These functions must be members of the class to be converted. They have names of the form `operator` *T* where *T* is a type name or specification of the type that is the conversion result.

   We add to `class String` a conversion operator to convert a `String` back to a `const char *`:

```
class String {
    char *str;
  public:
    operator const char*();
    // etc.
};


String::operator const char*() {
    return str;
}
```

The return type of `String::operator const char*()` is `const char*` and no other return type is specified in its declaration. Having the conversion operator return a `const` keeps the array pointed to by the member `str` from being written through the pointer returned by the conversion. The conversion operator can be used implicitly or with a cast.

```
String msg("Hello World");
const char *cp1, *cp2;

cp1 = (const char*)msg;
cp2 = msg;
printf("%s %s",cp1, cp2);
```

In the above, both `cp1` and `cp2` are set to the same value by the conversion of `msg` to `const char*`. Execution of the code fragment produces the output.

```
Hello World Hello World
```

3.8 Pointers to Class Members

Class members, other than `static` members, are components of class objects. The addresses of class data members are "offsets" relative to a particular object instance. The relative addresses of component class members are of type pointer to class member.

The type modifier for indicating a pointer to member in a declaration is $X::*$ where X is a class name. To dereference a pointer to member, operators `.*` and `->*` are used. Like their related member access operators, the pointer to member dereference operators must be used with a class type left operand.

In the following small examples, we declare, set, and use pointers to members of a simple class.

```
class Node {
  public:
    int code;
    int num;
    void print();
    void report();
};
```

First, the pointer to an `int` data member of `Node`:

```
int Node::*pi;

Node n, *np = new Node;
int i, j;

pi = &Node::code;
i = n.*pi;        // accesses n.code
j = np->*pi;      // accesses np->code

pi = &Node::num;
i = n.*pi;     // accesses n.num
j = np->*pi;      // accesses np->num
```

`pi` is declared to be a pointer to an `int` member of Node. It is set to point to `Node::code` and `Node::num` in turn, and is used to access these members of `Node` type objects.

The type specification of a pointer to function member is somewhat complex, so we use a `typedef` to give the name `Pftype` to the type pointer to function member of `Node` taking no arguments and returning `void`. We then declare pf as a pointer of this type.

```
typedef void ( Node::*Pftype )();
Pftype pf;

pf = &Node::print;
(n.*pf)();    // calls n.print()
(np->*pf)(); // calls np->print()

pf = &Node::report;
(n.*pf)();    // calls n.report()
(np->*pf)(); // calls np->report()
```

The pointer pf is used to call first Node::print and then Node::report for different Node objects. The parentheses are needed around the n.*pf and np->*pf to get the proper binding of the dereference operators over the call operator. Calling member functions in this way is the major use of pointers to members.

To demonstrate the use of a pointer to function member, we here extend the string-sort function to put the list in an ascending or descending order, depending on the value of an added third parameter. Member versions of String comparison operators are used.

```
class String {
    // hidden implementation
  public:
    // etc.
    int operator < ( String &s );
    int operator > ( String &s );
};
```

The function sort declares a variable compare as a pointer to a member function of String, taking a String argument and returning int. The variable compare is declared to be a pointer to the type of the functions between which we want to choose, and it is set to either String::operator > or String::operator <.

```
void sort( String *a, int n, int descending ) {
   int changed;

   typedef int ( String::* Ftype ) ( String );
   Ftype compare = descending ?
         String::operator > :
            String::operator <;
   do {
      changed = 0;
      for( int i = 0; i < n-1; i++ )
         if( ( a[i+1].*compare )( a[i] ) ) {
            // exchange array elements
         }
   } while( changed );
}
```

The function call through the pointer

```
( a[i+1].*compare )( a[i] )
```

is the same as either the infix operator function call

```
a[i+1] > a[i]
```

or

```
a[i+1] < a[i]
```

depending on the value of `compare`.

3.9 Exercises

Exercise 3-1. †Write a function that prints the bit representation of its `double` argument. □

Exercise 3-2. †Design a list class whose elements are `void` pointers. Provide operations to add a new element to the head or tail of the list, remove an element from the head of the list, and test if a list is empty. Will you supply these operations as member or non-member functions, as operator or non-operator functions? Give reasons for your decisions. □

Exercise 3-3. †Write a hash table class that stores and retrieves records with a character string key. Provide public member functions to insert, lookup, and remove records from the hash table. Hide the implementation details in the private part of the class. ☐

Exercise 3-4. Re-implement the hash table type of the previous exercise using a binary tree data structure without changing the public interface of the class. Are we still justified in calling the result a hash table type? If not, were we justified in calling the original implementation a hash table type? ☐

Exercise 3-5. Add a predicate search to the hash table type such that it returns success only if the record found also satisfies the predicate. Should this be implemented by overloading the lookup function or by providing a default argument? ☐

Exercise 3-6. Modify the predicate search of the previous exercise so that it can deal with "fuzzy" predicates that can return "true," "false," or "maybe" results. An item that produces a "maybe" result when a fuzzy predicate is applied is returned only if there is no item that produces a "true" result. ☐

Exercise 3-7. Modify the hash table type of the previous exercise so that it, and the records to which it refers, can be stored to disk and later retrieved. Examine your solution. What simplifying assumptions have you made about the records to which the hash table refers? ☐

Exercise 3-8. †Show how a runtime trace of block entry and exit can be accomplished using constructors and destructors. ☐

Exercise 3-9. The values of data members of a class object are volatile; they may be assigned new values during execution. Even const data members are initialized separately for each new object, and this initialization may take advantage of information obtained since the start of program execution.

The "values" of member functions, however, are fixed when the program is compiled. That is, a call of a member function with a given name and argument types will always result in the invocation of the same function. What are some advantages and disadvantages of this situation?

Design a way to implement member functions whose values (that is, the function invoked) may change during execution. What are the advantages and disadvantages of your solution as compared with the built-in C++ implementation of member functions? ☐

Exercise 3-10. In the previous exercise, each object of the class had its own functions, and these were changeable on a per-object basis. Modify your implementation so that the value of a member function may be changed simultaneously for all objects of a given class. ☐

Exercise 3-11. Show how one can use inline functions to provide ''read only'' class members. □

Exercise 3-12. Consider the following class definition.

```
class CharStar {
    char *cp;
  public:
    char *cp_val1() const
        { return cp; }
    const char *cp_val2() const
        { return cp; }
    // ...
};
```

Should `cp_val1` be a constant member function? Should `cp_val2`? □

Exercise 3-13. Show how member functions can be used to provide lazy evaluation of complex values. □

Exercise 3-14. †Give a verbal rendering of the following declarations, assuming that A, B, and C are class names:

```
int A::*a;
int A::*b();
int *A::*c;
int * A::* const d = 0;
int const * A::* const e = 0;
int A::*B::*f;
int A::**B::*C::**&g = 0;
int A::*(A::*h)(int A::*);
int (A::*i);
int (A::*j)();
```

□

Exercise 3-15. Use typedefs to simplify the declarations of the previous exercise. □

CHAPTER 4: **Data Abstraction**

An abstract data type is an encapsulated data type that is accessible only through an interface that hides the implementation details of the type. The properties of an abstract data type are defined by its interface and not by its internal structure, or implementation. The same abstract data type can, therefore, have different implementations at different times without affecting the code that uses it. It is in this sense that the data type is abstract: the properties of the type are defined by the interface, and the implementation details are abstracted away.

In C++, classes are used for data abstraction by hiding the implementation of a type in the private part of the class definition and providing an interface of publicly accessible operations. In this chapter, we present several examples of abstract data types implemented with C++ classes and discuss issues of designing classes for data abstraction.

4.1 Abstraction and Interface

The complex number class presented in Chapter 1 is a good example of an abstract data type.

```
class complex {
    double re, im;
  public:
    friend complex operator +( complex, complex );
    // ...
    friend complex operator /( complex, complex );
    complex( double = 0.0, double = 0.0 );
};
```

Since the abstract interface defines the semantics of the type for the user, an essential part of creating an abstract data type is the design of the interface. The design should reflect the abstract properties of the type and not simply prevent users from changing the implementation. This is the difference between protection, described in Chapter 3, and data abstraction. An interface that protects the implementation of a type from unauthorized access without hiding its structure can still allow the code that uses it to develop dependencies on the implementation.

For example, if the interface for our `complex` type revealed the implementation to be a pair of `doubles`, users of `complex` could write code based on the assumption that a complex number was implemented as a Cartesian coordinate pair.

```
class complex {
    // ...
    double first() { return re; }
    double second() { return im; }
};
extern complex a;
complex b( a.first(), a.second() );
```

If `complex` is implemented as a coordinate pair, then a equals b. If we change the implementation to a polar representation, `complex` is still implemented as a pair of `doubles`, but a is no longer necessarily equal to b.

For complex numbers, the essential semantics of the type are embodied in a set of arithmetic operations and conversions from and to other numeric types.

A complex number is a well-known abstract concept, and our users will have a well-defined concept of what an interface to a complex number data type should look like. Complex numbers can be added, subtracted, multiplied, and divided, so these properties are provided by overloading the operators +, −, *, and / to accept operands and produce results of type `complex`. It is not necessary to overload operators to provide this interface as non-operator functions with appropriate access permission can also be used to implement an abstract interface.

```
class complex {
    // ...
  public:
    friend complex add( complex, complex );
    // ...
    friend complex div( complex, complex );
    complex( double = 0, double = 0 );
};
```

The use of such functions for a complex number abstract data type, however, does not lead to a natural extension of the numeric types and operations already provided by the language. Compare

```
Z = add( add( R, mul( mul( j, omega ), L ) ),
         div( 1, mul( mul( j, omega ), C ) ) );
```

with the far more readable expression for AC impedance in Chapter 1.

```
Z = R + j * omega * L + 1/( j * omega * C );
```

Overloaded arithmetic operators provide an intuitive interface to class `complex`, but operator overloading can be abused. Since the semantics of the overloaded operator are determined by the implementer, it is possible to implement + to mean subtraction and – to mean addition, but in the absence of malicious intent it is unlikely that this will occur.

A more common abuse of operator overloading is overuse. For example, another property of complex numbers that should be represented in the abstract interface is exponentiation. Since C++ does not have an exponentiation operator, however, it is tempting to press an existing operator into service, such as ^ (exclusive or), that does not have a useful meaning for complex numbers. Although this is possible, this particular use of operator overloading will introduce bugs and harm readability. One reason for this is that the ^ operator already has a meaning that has nothing to do with exponentiation. A reader of a `complex` expression that employed ^ as an exponentiation operator is likely to assume instead that the expression involves, in some fashion, an exclusive or of complex numbers.

An additional reason is that ^ has the wrong precedence for exponentiation. A user of class `complex` might code the expression $-1 + e^{i\pi}$ as -1 + e^(i*pi), expecting the exponentiation operator to bind more tightly than addition, as it does in most languages that have a built-in exponentiation operator. Recall, however, that operator overloading does not change the existing precedences and associativities of operators, so the expression -1 + e^(i*pi) is interpreted as $(-1 + e)^{i\pi}$, because ^ has lower precedence than +. It is better in this case to abandon operator overloading for the more pedestrian but clearer use of a non-operator function.

```
-1 + pow( e, i*pi );
```

Operator overloading should be used only if the existing precedence and semantics of an operator support an intuitive understanding of its new use.

As we saw in Chapter 3, two kinds of functions have access to the private parts of a class definition: functions that are members of the class and functions that the class explicitly declares to be friends. Why did we choose to implement the arithmetic operations of complex numbers as friends rather than as members?

```
class complex {
    // ...
  public:
    // member operators
    complex operator +( complex );   // binary
    complex operator -( complex );   // binary
    complex operator -();  // unary
    // ...
};
```

The reason concerns the way in which complex numbers interact with other arithmetic types in mixed expressions.

As discussed in Chapter 3, the constructor for complex (which, like the operator functions, is part of the abstract interface) has a dual role. In addition to ensuring that every object of type complex is initialized, it also specifies a conversion from a value of type double to one of type complex. There are predefined conversions from the other arithmetic types to double; thus, the constructor also specifies a conversion to complex from the other predefined arithmetic types. The constructor is invoked implicitly to provide this conversion on assignment or initialization of a complex by a predefined arithmetic type.

```
complex x = 12.34;  // complex( 12.34, 0 )
x = 12;             // complex( (double)12, 0 )
```

Therefore, the constructor is invoked as necessary to perform conversions for the initialization of function formal arguments with the actual arguments of the call.

An operator function is not essentially different from a non-operator function and may be called either as an infix operator or as a non-operator function. Consider trying to write a `complex` expression that employs a member operator function.

```
complex a, b;
double c, d;
a + b;
a.operator +( b );  // fine...
a + d;
a.operator +( d );  // fine...
c + b;              // error!
c.operator +( b );  // error!
```

The trouble with the addition of c and b above is that we are attempting to call an operator function that is a member of the class of c, but c is not of class type and has no members! Whether it is written as c+b or as `c.operator +(b)` the expression makes no sense. If we had implemented the complex arithmetic operators as member functions, the users of our type could never write an expression in which the first operand of a complex operator was a noncomplex number without supplying an explicit conversion.

The implementation of operations on complex numbers by overloading the existing operators and by supplying initialization and conversion semantics with a constructor allows us to extend the arithmetic type system of C++ to include complex numbers that can be used as easily and as naturally as the built-in arithmetic types.

Data abstraction provides the ability to bring the programming language closer to a specific problem domain. The ability to define a `complex` data type gives users of complex numbers the ability to write compact, clear programs involving complex arithmetic because, in effect, the C++ language has been extended to aid the developer both to *think* and *code* in that problem area. This use of data abstraction as support for conceptual abstraction in program design is most important.

A complex number is a data type with such a wide range of applicability that it is a built-in type in many programming languages. Well-designed abstract data types, however, can confer similar advantages for more specialized application areas as well.

For instance, some applications may have need for a type that represents the semantics of a sorted collection of integers. Using the same approach we did for `complex` we define the public interface for such a type. Since we do not have an existing interface to copy, as in the case of complex numbers, we have simultaneously more freedom and greater responsibility for its design.

```
typedef int Etype;

class SortedCollection {
  public:
    SortedCollection();
    void insert( Etype );
    void apply( void (*)(Etype) );
};
```

This class represents a simple concept and, therefore, has a simple interface: there are operations to create a `SortedCollection`, insert a new integer into the collection, and apply a function to each element of the collection in sorted sequence.

We chose not to use operator functions to implement the interface to `SortedCollection` because it is not clear that their use would help a user of the type to understand the corresponding abstract operations; the intended meaning of the expression a + b is clear if a and b are complex numbers, but the meaning is less clear if a is a `SortedCollection` and b is an integer, and considerably less clear if a is a `SortedCollection` and b is a function pointer. Non-operator functions are much more commonly used than operator functions to implement abstract data type interfaces.

Now that the interface is defined, users of the type can start to design and code applications.

```
#include "scoll.h"

extern void print( int );
extern int read( int & );

void
printint() {
    // read in, sort and print some integers
    SortedCollection sc;
    int i;
    while( read( i ) )
        sc.insert( i );
    sc.apply( print );
}
```

A given abstraction may have many reasonable and effective interface designs but only a single actual interface as represented in the public part of a class definition. It is important to define a concrete interface that both communicates the abstraction to the user and reflects the user's needs.

4.2 Interface and Implementation

While users work with the interface to `SortedCollection`, we can complete a first implementation of it.

```
typedef int Etype;

class SortedCollection {
    Etype ary[ 100 ];
    int free; // next free slot
  public:
    SortedCollection()
        : free( 0 ) {}
    void insert( Etype );
    void apply( void (*)(Etype) );
};

void
SortedCollection::apply( void (*f)(Etype) ) {
    for( int i = 0; i != free; i++ )
        f( ary[ i ] );
}

void
SortedCollection::insert( Etype el ) {
    // Quick prototype, no checking!
    for( int i = free++; i && ary[ i-1 ] > el; i-- )
        ary[ i ] = ary[ i-1 ];
    ary[ i ] = el;
}
```

This implementation is clearly not very good. The insertion algorithm is inefficient for large collections. This inefficiency, however, is unlikely to cause problems because, long before it is noticeable, a large collection of integers will overrun the fixed-size collection array and bomb the program. The only positive point one can make about the implementation is that it took only a few minutes to write. This is advantage enough, because now users of the type can compile and begin to debug their applications while we work on providing a better implementation. Quick implementations like this are useful in the initial design stages of a programming project, when the public interface to an abstract data type has not yet been fixed. In this way, users can experiment with the type and request modifications to its interface without causing any expensively-produced code to be invalidated.

We now refine our implementation in order to handle large collections correctly and efficiently.

```
typedef int Etype;

class SortedCollection {
  public:
    SortedCollection();
    ~SortedCollection();
    void insert( Etype );
    void apply( void (*)(Etype) );
  private:
    class Tree { // binary tree
        Etype el;
        Tree *lchild, *rchild;
        Tree( Etype i )
           : el( i ), lchild( 0 ), rchild( 0 ) {}
        ~Tree()
           { delete lchild; delete rchild; }
        void insert( Etype );
        void apply( void (*)(Etype) );   // inorder
        friend class SortedCollection;
    } *root;
    SortedCollection( SortedCollection & ); // See 7.3
    void operator =( SortedCollection & ); // See 7.3
};

inline
SortedCollection::SortedCollection()
    : root( 0 ) {}

inline
SortedCollection::~SortedCollection()
    { delete root; }
```

```
inline void
SortedCollection::insert( Etype el ) {
   if( root )
      root->insert( el );
   else
      root = new Tree( el );
}

inline void
SortedCollection::apply( void (*f)(Etype) )
   { if( root ) root->apply( f ); }
```

Since this implementation of SortedCollection is significantly more complex than the previous version, we have moved the public interface to the start of the class and moved some of the inline function definitions outside the class. In this way, users of the class can discern at a glance the essential information about the abstract type. We have also employed a private, nested class in the implementation of the type. This encapsulation prevents other classes from developing dependencies on the implementation of SortedCollection which, in turn, would restrict our ability to change the implementation should the need arise. Note that it was was necessary to declare SortedCollection to be a friend of SortedCollection::Tree. A class has no special access privileges to classes scoped within it.

```
void
SortedCollection::Tree::insert( Etype i ) {
   if( i < el )
      if( lchild )
         lchild->insert( i );
      else
         lchild = new Tree( i );
   else
      if( rchild )
         rchild->insert( i );
      else
         rchild = new Tree( i );
}
```

```
void
SortedCollection::Tree::apply( void (*f)(Etype) ) {
    if( lchild )
        lchild->apply( f );
    f( el );
    if( rchild )
        rchild->apply( f );
}
```

Our second implementation is better than the first in that it can handle large collections, and element insertion is much more efficient. Unless they run up against one of the limitations of the first implementation, however, users of the type cannot distinguish between implementations. Each implementation is just a different representation of the same abstract type, and the abstract semantics are unchanged from one implementation to the other.

This is not to say that these "secondary," or implementation-specific, semantics cannot have a profound effect on the behavior of programs that use the type. Our initial implementation of SortedCollection has the implicit assumption that no user program will attempt to insert more than 100 integers in a given collection. Since this limitation is not represented in the abstract interface, however, users of the type are not aware of it and may violate the restriction.

More insidious are situations in which programs take advantage of implementation-specific semantics that are not explicitly part of the abstract semantics of a type. For example, we can create a collection data type (whose elements do not *have* to be sorted) from a sorted collection.

```
typedef SortedCollection Collection;
```

Unfortunately, a user of this type can write a program that takes advantage of the fact that the collection just happens to be sorted. Later, we may reimplement Collection to do more efficient insertions than SortedCollection by not sorting, effectively invalidating programs that depend on the implementation-specific semantics.

For these reasons, it is often useful to view the public interface to an abstract data type as a contract between implementer and user of the type. The implementer is required to supply the correct abstract semantics specified by the interface without making any unnecessary additional assumptions, and users of the type should assume only those semantics explicitly present in the public interface.

Notice also that we have added a destructor to the public interface of `SortedCollection` for the second implementation. The previous implementation did not require an explicit destructor because objects of the class were entirely self-contained. This second implementation, however, causes a binary tree to be constructed outside the class object as elements are added to the collection; the destructor ensures that this extra-object storage is reclaimed when the `SortedCollection` object itself is destroyed.

It is a good idea to keep in mind the concept of the *object lifecycle* while designing the implementation of an abstract data type. When an object comes into existence, it must be properly initialized by a constructor; while it is in use, its member and friend functions must leave it in a consistent state; when it is destroyed, its destructor must properly reclaim any resources allocated during its lifetime.

As a further example of data abstraction, let us look at a modified version of the `String` data type of Chapter 3.

```
class String {
  public:
    String( const char * = "" );
    ~String();
    String( const String & );
    operator const char *() const;
    String &operator =( const String & );
    friend String operator +(  const String &, const String & );
    String &operator +=( const String & );
    friend int operator <( const String &, const String & );
    // other relational and equality operators...
  private:
    class Rep {
        char *str;
        int refs; // reference count
        Rep( const char * );
        ~Rep();
        friend class String;
    } *r;  // -> shared, ref-counted string
};
```

In this version of the `String` class we have decided to share the actual character strings as much as possible and have created a class, `String::Rep`, that binds together a character string and a reference count. The String class now refers to this data structure instead of referring directly to the character string.

The first constructor is very simple, specifying how to initialize a String with a character string (and, as with any constructor that can be invoked with a single argument, specifies a conversion from the argument type to the class type).

```
String::String( const char *s )
    : r( new Rep( s ) ) {}
```

Class String::Rep takes care of its own initialization.

```
String::Rep::Rep( const char *s )
    : str( strcpy(new char[strlen(s)+1],s) ), refs(1) {}
```

When one String is initialized with another, instead of creating a second copy of the character string, we refer to the existing representation and increment its reference count. We specify these semantics with a constructor that can be invoked with a single String& argument.

```
String::String( const String &init )
    : r( init.r ) { r->refs++; }
```

The semantics of assignment are similar, but we must also be concerned about the String::Rep to which the left operand (the target) of the assignment referred before being assigned its new value. The reference count of the String::Rep is decremented because the String that is the target of the assignment will no longer refer to it. If there are no references remaining, the String::Rep is deleted.

```
String &
String::operator =( const String &str ) {
    if( this != &str ) {
        if( !--r->refs )
            delete r;
        r = str.r;
        r->refs++;
    }
    return *this;
}
```

To parallel the behavior of the built-in assignment operator, the assignment operator for String not only changes the target of the assignment, but also returns the lvalue of the object, allowing assignments to be "chained": a=b=c. The `this` pointer is used to access the object in order to return its lvalue. We also take care to check the possibility of assignment of an object to itself. Otherwise we could delete the `String::Rep` object and later attempt to assign its address to `r`.

Note the difference in semantics of assignment and initialization between `String`s and complex numbers. In the case of our implementation of complex numbers, the predefined semantics of assignment and initialization are sufficient, and the representation of one complex number is simply copied member by member into another. In order to have a correct implementation of `String`s, the reference count in the `Rep` to which the `String` refers must be updated on assignment. It is necessary to provide `operator = ` for class `String`.

In general, if it is necessary to supply assignment for an abstract data type, it is a good idea also to supply initialization and vice versa. In the `String` type, supplying one without the other would cause as much trouble as their omission altogether. Together, these operations specify how objects of a given class type are to be copied in all situations. We will have more to say about copy semantics in Chapter 7.

We must also take care to adjust reference counts for `String`s that are deleted or that go out of scope. For this we define a destructor.

```
String::~String()
    { if( !--r->refs ) delete r; }
```

As in the complex number type, we have supplied overloaded operators and a constructor in order to interface well with the existing type system of C++. One of the constructors supplies a conversion from character strings to `String`s, and the concatenation operation is supplied by overloading operator + as a friend, as are the complex arithmetic operators.

```
extern char *home_dir, *path, *file;
String home = home_dir;
String fpath = home + "/" + path + "/" + file;
```

To complete the interface of the `String` type with the existing type system, we supply an operator that defines a conversion from a `String` to a `char *`. In this conversion operator we take the efficient but potentially dangerous approach of returning the address of the private character string rather than the address of a copy of the string. We are returning the address of a string of constant characters, however, so users will have to cast the return value to modify the characters. Data hiding in C++ is a means to guard against accident, but is not proof against willful misuse.

```
String::operator const char *() const
   { return r->str; }
// ...
char *newfile = fpath; // fpath.operator const char *()
```

This conversion in effect supplies the inverse function of a constructor. The `String` class's constructors specify how to create a `String` from a `char *` or another `String`, whereas the conversion operator `operator const char *` specifies how to create a `char *` from a `String`. This capability is important for completing the interface to the existing C++ type system in that it provides for an interface to existing code written for objects of type `char *`.

```
extern FILE *fopen( const char *, const char * );
FILE *fp = fopen( fpath, "r+" );
```

As with a constructor, the conversion operator is invoked implicitly as required in expressions and initializers.

Unlike the overloaded + operator for concatenation, and unlike the complex arithmetic operators, we have implemented the `String` assignment operators as member functions. The reason for doing so is that the "handedness" engendered by members with respect to automatic argument conversion is precisely what is required for assignment; we do not want conversions applied to the left argument of an assignment. In fact, C++ requires that `operator =` be a member function; there is, however, no such restriction on other assignment operators.

If `operator +=` were implemented as a friend function, it would then be possible to assign `String`s to character strings, because the `char *` on the left side of the assignment would be automatically converted to a `String` by the `String` constructor that accepts a `const char *` argument.

```
"/usr/bin" += pathname;
```

Recall that the use of overloaded infix operators is just a notational convenience and is entirely equivalent to a function call.

```
operator +=( "/usr/bin", pathname );
```

Therefore, although we probably do not want to allow assignments to character string literals like `"/usr/bin"` this is, nevertheless, correct if `operator +=` is not a member of class `String`. In making `+=` a member function, the assignment above makes as much sense as

```
"/usr/bin".operator +=( pathname );
```

that is, it makes no sense at all. Implementing `String` assignment as a member function prevents such conversions from being applied to the left operand of the assignment. The more reasonable semantics of assigning or initializing a `const char *` with a `String` are already handled by the conversion operator `operator const char *`.

The proper use of operator functions, constructors, and conversion operators allows us to design abstract data types that merge with and extend the predefined type system of C++.

Data abstraction confers two major, and equally important, advantages on its users. First, it simplifies the semantics of using a type to what is explicitly represented in the public interface. Users of the type do not have to contend with implementation-dependent semantics that have no meaning for the abstract function of the type. For example, users of the `String` type do not have to worry about maintaining reference counts when doing assignments or overflowing buffers when doing concatenations. These ''secondary'' semantics are the property of the hidden implementation and are the responsibility of the implementer of the type. By the same token, the implementer is free to change the implementation without fear of affecting the meaning of user code as long as the abstract semantics of the type are preserved.

4.3 Control Abstraction

The `apply` function of class `SortedCollection` is really a composition of two separate concepts: traversal of whatever data structure is used to hold the elements of a `SortedCollection` and applying a function to an element of the collection. Both of these concepts, as well as their composition as in the `apply` function, belong to a general class of abstractions that we call control abstractions.

Traversal of the hidden representation of a data structure without any attendant operation is clearly of little use. If the traversal can be broken up into stages, however, each of which yields some interesting value, then users of the type can access values associated with the type in a way that preserves the privacy of the hidden implementation. A control abstraction of this kind is called an *iterator*.

Consider the implementation of a list type. A list has a head, a tail, and a sequence of elements in between. We would like to design a mechanism that gives access to the values of the list elements in sequence. We can not easily embed traversal operations within the list itself, however, since this would preclude the existence of multiple, simultaneous traversals of the list.

An alternate design makes a clean separation between structuring and traversal semantics by encapsulating structuring operations in a list class, and traversal operations in a separate control abstraction class.

```
class List {
  public:
    List();
    ~List();
    void append( Etype );
    friend class ListIter;
  private:
    struct Node {
        Node *next;
        Etype el;
    } *head, *tail;
};

class ListIter {
  public:
    ListIter( const List & ); // set to first
    int done() const;        // iteration finished?
    Etype get() const;       // current element
    void next();             // move to next
  private:
    List::Node *current;
};
```

Here we have designed an iterator type, associated with a list type, that embodies the control abstraction of sequencing through the elements of a list in the same way that a list embodies the abstraction of the list data structure. To iterate through the elements of a list, we create an iteration object and bind it to a list object on initialization. The public interface of the list iterator is designed with an eye toward its intended use in a loop construct.

```
void
print_list( const List &seq ) {
    for( ListIter i = seq; !i.done(); i.next() )
        print( i.get() );
}
```

The essential idea is that the iterator object has a concept of the state of the iteration that it retains from invocation to invocation. This state is maintained separately from the state of the list on which the iteration is performed, allowing multiple iterations to be performed on the same list without interference.

```
inline
ListIter::ListIter( const List &ilist )
    : current( ilist.head ) {}

inline int
ListIter::done() const
    { return current == 0; }

inline Etype
ListIter::get() const
    { return current->el; }

inline void
ListIter::next()
    { if( current ) current = current->next; }
```

The iterator is, in effect, an extension of the list class that provides abstract flow-of-control operations. This creation of abstract flow-of-control types that are applied in conjunction with abstract data types is a powerful mechanism for working with abstract types with complex internal structure in an implementation-independent manner.

Note that a `ListIter` object can be used to initialize or assign to another `ListIter` object.

```
void
ripple( const List &list ) {
    for( ListIter i = list; !i.done(); i.next() ) {
        for( ListIter j = i; !j.done(); j.next() )
            print( j.get() );
        print( '\n' );
    }
}
```

The iterator for our list class is very simple. We could have implemented more complex semantics, however. For instance, creation of an iterator for a list could have the side effect of locking the list so no new elements can be inserted until the iteration is complete. We could have defined more general motion on lists. For instance, we could add a scanning function to class `ListIter` that returns the next list element that satisfies an argument predicate function, or we could add the ability to backup to the previous element or to the head of the list. Multiple iterator types can be created for the same abstract data type.

```
class Employee {
    // ...
  public:
    int isMgr();
    int isTrue()
        { return 1; }
};

extern void print( Employee * );
extern void fire( Employee * );
typedef Employee *Etype;

class List {
    // ...
};
```

```
class ListCtl {
  public:
    ListCtl( const List & );
    ~ListCtl();
    typedef int (Employee::*MemPred)() const;
    typedef int (*NonmemPred)(const Employee &);
    Etype operator()();      // next
    Etype operator()( MemPred ); // next satisfying predicate
    Etype operator()( NonmemPred ); // next satisfying predicate
  private:
    // ...
};

void
down_size( List &alist, int all ) {
    ListCtl next = alist;
    Employee *e;
    while( e = next() )
        print( e );
    int (Employee::*criterion)()
        = all ? &Employee::isTrue : &Employee::isMgr;
    ListCtl next_victim = alist;
    while( e = next_victim( criterion );
        fire( e );
}
```

The two central ideas behind control abstraction are the same as those discussed earlier in this chapter for data abstraction in general. First, the user of a control abstraction is unaffected by the details of its implementation. In addition to reducing the amount of knowledge that must be acquired before a user can write a simple flow-of-control structure, the implementer of a type can change its implementation (and the implementation of the type's associated control abstractions) without affecting user code.

Second, control abstraction brings the programming language closer to the control aspects of the problem in the same way that data abstraction does for the type aspects. This is especially valuable in more complex situations, in which the concept of what is going on would otherwise be lost in the details of its implementation.

There is no obvious dividing line between control and data abstraction, or between abstract and nonabstract data types, nor should there be. The use of data abstraction is an opportunity to unleash your imagination to determine the data types with which your problem deals. Integers, complex numbers, strings, lists, communication networks, telephones, and grammars all have (at least as far as programs are concerned) abstract properties that can be represented in the public interface to an abstract data type. Data abstraction is also an invitation to create new implementations of these types and control structures to make working with them natural.

4.4 Genericity

A sorted collection of integers is a useful data type for certain applications, but so are sorted collections of `doubles`, `Strings`, and even sorted collections. It is clear that the abstraction with which we are concerned is a sorted collection in general, and not a sorted collection of objects of any one type. What we would like to be able to do is parameterize our implementation of `SortedCollection` and then instantiate, or create, instances of it for specific element types. In this way, a single parameterized implementation of `SortedCollection` can serve as a generic representation of the semantics of sorted collections. Each instantiation will produce a new sorted collection type for a specified element type. Users will then be able to declare and use objects of these instantiated types.

Consider our second implementation of `SortedCollection`. We have actually implemented the type to work with elements of type `Etype`, where `Etype` has been defined with a `typedef` to be an `int`. What properties of `Etype` are used by our implementation? Looking through the code, we find that an `Etype` must have the operators = and < defined for it, and it must be possible to initialize one `Etype` with another (in order to initialize the `Etype` formal argument of the function pointer in `SortedCollection::apply`). Simply changing the `typedef` to define `Etype` as some other type with these properties will, in effect, instantiate a version of `SortedCollection` for the given `Etype`.

```
typedef String Etype;
class SortedCollection {
    // ...
};

extern void print( const char * );
extern void censor( char * );
extern char *readstr();

void
printString() {
    // sort and print the input sentences,
    // removing objectionable text
    SortedCollection list;
    char *s;
    while( s = readstr() )
        list.insert( s );
    list.apply( censor );
    list.apply( print );
}
```

(Note how the implicit conversions described earlier in this chapter from `String` to `char *` and vice versa are employed above.)

This scheme works well if we need no more than one sorted collection type but it cannot be used for multiple instantiations. An `Etype` cannot be two types simultaneously! The use of class templates addresses this problem.

```
template <class Etype>
class SCollection {
    // ...
  public:
    SCollection();
    ~SCollection();
    void insert( Etype );
    void apply( void (*)( Etype ) );
};
```

The keyword `template` and its associated template parameters introduce a class template in the same way that they do a function template, as described in Chapter 2.

Users can now instantiate versions of the generic sorted collection class and declare objects of the instantiated types. Just as a template member function is instantiated implicitly by calling a function, a class template is instantiated implicitly by using its name. A template class name is composed of the name of the class template followed by one or more parameters enclosed by angle brackets.

```
SCollection<int> ints;
```

This declaration instantiates a version of SCollection that contains integers, and creates an object of that type. A typedef can be used to supply an alternative, more readable name for an instantiated template type.

```
typedef SCollection<int> SCInt;
SCInt ints;
```

Users can now instantiate versions of our generic sorted collection template and declare objects of the instantiated types.

```
#include "scolltmp.h"
#include "String.h"

extern void print( int );
extern void print( String );
extern int read( int & );
extern char *readstr();
extern void censor( String );

void
printint() {
    // ...
    SCollection<int> sc;
    int i;
    while( read( i ) )
        sc.insert( i );
    sc.apply( print );
}
```

```
void
printString() {
    // ...
    SCollection<String> list;
    char *s;
    while( s = readstr() )
        list.insert( s );
    list.apply( censor );
    list.apply( print );
}
```

We base our implementation of the `SCollection` template on the second implementation of the `SortedCollection` class shown earlier in this chapter.

```
#include "tree.h"

template <class Etype>
class SCollection {
    Tree<Etype> *root;
  public:
    SCollection() : root( 0 ) {}
    ~SCollection() { delete root; }
    void insert( Etype el ) {
        if( root ) root->insert( el )
        else root = new Tree<Etype>( el ); }
    void apply( void (*f)(Etype) )
        { if( root ) root->apply( f ); }
};
```

Note that this implementation makes use of another class template, `Tree`. The implementation of the `Tree` template is based on our earlier implementation of the `SortedCollection::Tree` class.

```
template <class T>
class Tree {
    T el;
    Tree<T> *lchild, *rchild;
    Tree( T );
    ~Tree();
    void insert( T );
    void apply( void (*)(T) );
    friend class SCollection<T>;
};
```

The member functions of a class template are defined in a similar manner to non-member template functions.

```
template <class T>
Tree<T>::Tree( T i )
    : el( i ), lchild( 0 ), rchild( 0 ) {}

template <class T>
Tree<T>::~Tree()
    { delete lchild; delete rchild; }

template <class T>
void Tree<T>::apply( void (*f)(T) ) {
    if( lchild )
        lchild->apply( f );
    f( el );
    if( rchild )
        rchild->apply( f );
}
```

By proceeding in a manner analogous to the above, it is possible to define and use generic types that require more than a single type parameter for instantiation.

4.5 Exercises

Exercise 4-1. Change the implementation of class `complex` to use polar coordinates instead of (real, imaginary) pairs. How does this change affect client code? □

Exercise 4-2. Should class `complex` provide a member, `operator double()`, to provide automatic conversions from complex numbers to the predefined arithmetic types? □

Exercise 4-3. Create a new integral type, `VeryLong`, which has four times the capacity of a `long`. Define overloaded operators and conversions to merge it with the existing type system. Will you allow a `VeryLong` to be converted to a `long`? If not, will you allow a `VeryLong` value as the conditional value in an if-statement or as a switch-expression? Why or why not? What would the users of the type expect? Do they know what is good for them, or should you decide? □

Exercise 4-4. Design a rational number type that implements rational numbers of unbounded size and precision. Provide overloaded arithmetic operators and conversions to merge the new type with the existing type system. □

Exercise 4-5. †Design a stack of integers type. What operations should be available for the stack? Should these operations be implemented as members or non-members, as overloaded operators or non-operator functions? □

Exercise 4-6. Re-implement the stack type of the previous exercise as a generic stack type by using a template. Use your template to instantiate a stack of stacks of integers class. □

Exercise 4-7. Design and implement a bounded sorted collection, similar in functionality to the sorted collection type of this chapter, but able to contain only a fixed maximum number of elements. Base your implementation on the first implementation of `SortedCollection` in this chapter, but keep in mind the object lifecycle in your design. □

Exercise 4-8. Re-implement the `List`, `ListIter`, and `ListCtl` types of this chapter with a circular list. Do not change the abstract interfaces of the types. □

Exercise 4-9. Re-implement the `List`, `ListIter`, and `ListCtl` classes of this chapter as class templates parameterized by element type. □

Exercise 4-10. †Modify the list-of-pointers type of Exercise 3-2 so that it can be instantiated for any pointer type. □

Exercise 4-11. Consider a date abstract data type with the following interface:

```
class Date {
  public:
    Date( char * );
    Date( int, int, int );
    const char *str();
    Date &operator ++();
    Date &operator --();
    friend int operator ==( const Date &, const Date & );
    friend int operator !=( const Date &, const Date & );
    friend int operator <( const Date &, const Date & );
    // etc.
};
```

A `Date` is initialized either with a character string representation of a date such as `17 June 1775` or by three integers representing day, month, and year: `17, 6, 1775`. The conversion operator returns a pointer to a character string representation of the date. The `++` and `--` operators increment and decrement the date by one day, respectively.

Provide three different implementations of this abstract data type, using a single integer, three integers, and a character string to implement the internal form of a date. What are the relative merits of each implementation? What are the merits of having a single abstract type for all three implementations? □

Exercise 4-12. †Note that the interface to the `Date` class above would permit usage of the form

```
Date d( 17, 6, 1775 );
// ...
if( d < "2 July 1776" ) {
    // ...
```

Design a technique to prevent such conversions of character strings to `Date`s in comparisons, but still retain the ability to initialize a `Date` with a character string. □

Exercise 4-13. Most calculations relating to physical systems are not composed solely of scalar operands; they also contain operands with associated physical units. For example, the calculation of AC impedance involves calculation with elements in ohms, farads, and so forth. It is a useful check when doing such calculations to carry the algebraic operations through on the physical unit types as well as on the numeric values of the operands. The calculated physical unit type should match the expected result type. Design integer, floating point, and complex data types that include associated physical units. Overload the arithmetic operators to calculate both the correct arithmetic and physical unit of the result. Provide conversions between the types and the predefined and complex arithmetic types. □

Exercise 4-14. †Implement operators +, +=, and < for the `String` type of this chapter. □

Exercise 4-15. Design a directed graph data type and consider the following points: Is the representation hidden? Is the interface as small and clean as possible? On the other hand, is the interface rich enough to allow users of the type to write useful procedures? □

Exercise 4-16. Write a control abstraction for the graph abstract data type above that follows the sequence of nodes for a set of depth first spanning trees for the graph. □

Exercise 4-17. Design a finite state automaton data type. What is the set of initializers for this type? What error conditions should be detected when constructing the type? What are the uses of such a type? Can a single representation serve for both the directed graph abstraction and the FSA? Why or why not, and what are the relative advantages of having a single representation or two representations? □

Exercise 4-18. †Design and implement an appropriate control abstraction for the `SortedCollection` type of this chapter. Base your implementation on the first, array based implementation of `SortedCollection`. ⊔

Exercise 4-19. Re-implement your solution to the previous exercise to work with the second, tree-based, implementation of `SortedCollection`. □

Exercise 4-20. †Design a binary tree type with operations to create, insert an element, look up a value, and destroy. Include a traversal that applies a function to each element in inorder sequence. □

Exercise 4-21. †Design an inorder control abstraction for the binary tree type of the previous exercise that returns the next element in sequence on each invocation. □

Exercise 4-22. Design a generic array type that performs bounds checking. □

Exercise 4-23. Rewrite the `String` type to dispense with reference counting, taking care not to change the abstract interface. Is the constructor `String(const String&)` still necessary? How about `operator =`? □

Exercise 4-24. Given the context

```
String salut = "Hello, world.";

void
excitement( char *s ) {
    for( ; *s; s++ )
        if( *s == '.' )
            *s = '!';
}
```

what meaning might one assign to the following statements?

```
String yo = salut + excitement;
String yoyo = salut + " Goodbye, cruel world."
        + excitement + "...";
```

Change the definition of `String` to make the above statements both legal and useful. □

Exercise 4-25. Design a histogram data type by overloading `operator[]` to index with floating arguments. □

Exercise 4-26. †Design an associative array type for a dictionary (mapping `String=>String`). Make the type generic by supplying type parameters for both index and element type of the array. What other useful types might be instantiated from this generic associative array type? □

Exercise 4-27. †Design a two-way list whose implementation uses only a single link pointer. Include in your design a control abstraction that can traverse the list in either direction. □

Exercise 4-28. Modify the definition of `SortedCollection` to allow a collection to be indexed with a predicate function. The result of the index operation is a new collection that contains the elements of the indexed collection that satisfy the predicate. □

Exercise 4-29. Design a "delayed execution" type that allows the construction of a sequence of actions that are later applied to an object. Provide the ability to bind an object of a given type to the delayed execution object so that both the sequence of actions and the object on which to perform them can be passed as an argument. What could be the use of such a type? □

Exercise 4-30. Examine Exercise 3-2 and its solution. What important abstract properties of the list type have not been specified in the statement of the problem, and how have these properties been implemented in the solution? How else might they have been implemented, and how would a user of the list type been affected by such a reimplementation? □

class scope if the name is not found. In cases in which one wants to access a base class member hidden by a derived class member with the same spelling, the syntax `base::member` can be used to specify that name lookup start in the scope of `base`. For example, if `p` is of type `List2El *`, then `p->ListEl::link` refers to the `link` data member inherited from the `ListEl` base class, and not to the `link` data member declared in `List2El`.

The function `whatsbefore` accesses both inherited and regular members in the same way.

```
List2El *
whatsbefore( List2El *lst, Etype e ) {
    for( List2El *p = lst; p; p = (List2El *)p->next() )
        if( p->value() == e )
            break;
    if( p )
        return p->previous();
    else
        return 0;
}
```

Nested class scope explains why this code works. Only the call to `previous` refers to a member explicitly declared in `List2El`. The calls to `next` and `value` refer to base class member functions inherited from `ListEl`.

Alternatively, we could have supplied `List2El` with a full complement of member functions for list traversal and access to the element value.

```
class List2El : public ListEl {
    List2El *link;
  public:
    List2El( Etype, List2El * = 0, List2El * = 0 );
    ListEl *next() const;
    List2El *previous() const;
    Etype value() const;
};
```

Unfortunately, we soon run into problems. Consider the implementation of `List2El::next`.

```
ListEl *
List2El::next() const {
    return ListEl::link;    // error!
}
```

Here we attempt to return the value of the forward link from the base class. This is an error, however, because `ListEl::link` is private. Unless it is declared to be a friend, a derived class does not have any special access privileges to its base class's private members. Our only choice is to use `ListEl`'s public interface to access the value

```
return ListEl::next();
```

which will work but hardly seems worth the effort when the same behavior is obtained by doing nothing at all.

Recall that the class definition for `List2El` started with

```
class List2El : public ListEl
```

The keyword `public` in this context specifies that the public members of `ListEl` will also be public to users of `List2El`. If the keyword `private` were used, then the public members of `ListEl` would be private when accessed through `List2El`. For example, in function `whatsbefore` all references to `value` and `next` would be erroneous references to private members. Note that the members and friends of `List2El` have access to the public members of `ListEl` whether or not it is a public or private base class.

Derived class constructors can include explicit initialization of a base class in the member initialization list. The constructor for `List2El` uses a member initialization list to initialize its base class, just as it would initialize a member. The initialization of a base class is entirely analogous to initialization of class members described in Chapter 3, except that a base class is always initialized before any member, even if a member initializer appears before the base class initializer on the member initialization list. If a base class has no constructor, it need not be initialized. If a base class has a constructor that can be invoked without arguments, it need not be explicitly initialized, but it will be initialized implicitly.

```
List2El::List2El( Etype e, List2El *fl, List2El *bl )
    : ListEl( e, fl ), link( bl ) {}
```

The arguments supplied to the base class constructor in the member initialization list of the `List2El` constructor are of type `Etype` and `List2El` `*`, whereas the types expected by the `ListEl` constructor are `Etype` and `ListEl` `*`. Why is it not an error to initialize a `ListEl` `*` with a `List2El` `*`? The reason is that an object of class `List2El` is also an object of class `ListEl`. This is what we specify when we derive one class from another. Additionally, if a class `Base` is a *public* base class of another class `Derived`, then there is a predefined conversion from a `Derived` to a `Base`, from a pointer to a `Derived` to a pointer to a `Base`, and from a reference to a `Derived` to a reference to a `Base`. We say that a `Derived` *is a* `Base` in many contexts. These conversions do not exist if `Base` is a private base class of `Derived`.

This "is-a" concept is a powerful abstraction mechanism, in that it allows derived classes to be treated as base classes in many contexts. For example, because `ListEl` is a public base class of `List2El`, we can call a function that expects a list composed of `ListEl`s with either a list composed of `ListEl`s or a list composed of `List2El`s.

```
typedef int Etype;

void
print_list( ListEl *lst ) {
    extern void print( int );
    for( ListEl *p = lst; p; p = p->next() )
        print( p->value() );
}

main() {
    ListEl *lp = new ListEl( 3 );
    lp = new ListEl( 2, lp );
    lp = new ListEl( 1, lp );
    print_list( lp );

    List2El *l2p = new List2El( 3 );
    l2p = new List2El( 2, l2p );
    l2p = new List2El( 1, l2p );
    print_list( l2p );
}
```

5.2 Augmentation and Specialization

In some cases, a derived class may just add or modify behavior of its base class. For instance, in the previous chapter we used the `String` type to create a pathname for a file and open it. We can encapsulate this behavior in a class derived from `String`.

The abstract operations we want to perform on pathnames are creation, concatenation, and comparison of the character strings that represent the pathname, as well as an ''open'' operation on the files to which they refer. Many of these operations are provided in the `String` type, and a pathname can be viewed as either an augmentation or a special case of `String`. When we say, ''A pathname is a `String` with the following additional properties . . . ,'' we are thinking of an augmented `String`. When we say, ''A pathname is a kind of `String` that . . .,'' we are thinking of a special case of a `String`. Whichever of these conceptualizations we use, we express it with class derivation.

```
class Pathname : public String {
  public:
    friend Pathname
        operator +( const Pathname &, const Pathname & );
    Pathname &operator +=( const Pathname & );
    FILE *open();
};
```

In this case, we are not adding any data members to what `Pathname` inherits from `String`, we are just adding behavior. In this sense, a `Pathname` is simply a `String` viewed from a different perspective.

We inherit the data members, the comparison operations, and the conversion to `const char *` unchanged from `String`. For concatenation, however, it is necessary to separate two sequences of directory names with a slash.

```
Pathname
operator +( const Pathname &p1, const Pathname &p2 )
    { return (const String &)p1 + "/" + p2; }
```

`Pathname::open` attempts to open the file referred to by the `String` representation of the pathname.

```
FILE *
Pathname::open()
   { return fopen( *this, "r+" ); }
```

The `Pathname` actual argument to `fopen` is converted to a `const char *` by the `operator const char *` inherited from class `String`.

While ordinary base class member functions are inherited by derived classes, constructors and destructors are not. In the case of `Pathname`, the compiler recognizes that a constructor and destructor are necessary (in order to initialize and clean up the `String` base class part of `Pathname`), and supplies default versions of these functions for us as if we had explicitly supplied a public inline constructor with no member initialization list and an empty body, as well as a public inline destructor with an empty body.

```
class Pathname : public String {
  public:
    Pathname() {}
    ~Pathname() {}
    // ...
};
```

The compiler-supplied constructor will behave correctly, invoking the `String` constructor with its default argument, but the result may surprise the user of `Pathname`.

```
Pathname deadend = "/usr/bin";   // error!
Pathname empty;           // OK...
```

In this case, it is probably best to provide a `Pathname` constructor and destructor explicitly.

```
class Pathname : public String {
  public:
    Pathname( const char *s = "" ) : String( s ) {}
    Pathname( const String &s ) : String( s ) {}
    ~Pathname() {}
    // ...
};
```

```
extern char *home_dir, *path, *file;
Pathname home = home_dir;
Pathname file = home + path + file;
FILE *fp = file.open();
```

This example illustrates one of the central ideas in using derived classes: inherit most of a class's behavior from base classes, and add to base class behavior only when necessary. Inheritance used in this way is an effective technique for sharing and reusing code.

5.3 Class Hierarchies

Many problems are not easily modeled as distinct types but are more naturally represented as collections of related types. For example, a node for a compiler abstract syntax tree may have to represent a variety of programming language constructs. Each of these types of node shares a common core of properties with the others (those properties that make them nodes), but each kind of node has additional properties that distinguish it from the others. Using only data abstraction to represent all node types gives us the choice of creating either a single type that incorporates the complexities of all the others or a set of distinct types that does not reflect their commonality. A better approach is to use class derivation to create a set of node types related by inheritance.

We approach this problem by creating a hierarchy of node types. The base class types in the hierarchy provide the common structure and functionality, and, conversely, the derived class types provide specialized versions of their base classes.

Suppose we are designing an abstract syntax tree for a calculator program. Each internal node of the tree represents an operation to be performed, and each leaf represents a value. For example, the expression -11+21*93 would be represented as

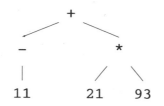

if the operators +, *, and unary - have the same precedences in our calculator language as they do in C++.

We start by defining a general node type that serves as a base class for all other node types.

```
class Node {
    const int code;
  public:
    enum { PLUS, TIMES, UMINUS, INT };
    Node( int c ) : code( c ) {}
    int eval() const;
};
```

Node contains a code that identifies the actual type of node (+, *, unary –, or integer), a constructor, and a member function to evaluate an abstract syntax tree.

We use class derivation to create distinct node types from Node for the operators +, *, and unary –, and for the integer values at the leaves of the tree. The derived class constructors explicitly invoke the base class constructor and supply the appropriate node code.

```
class Plus : public Node {
  public:
    Node *left, *right;
    Plus( Node *1, Node *r )
        : Node( PLUS ), left( 1 ), right( r ) {}
};

class Times : public Node {
  public:
    Node *left, *right;
    Times( Node *1, Node *r )
        : Node( TIMES ), left( 1 ), right( r ) {}
};

class Uminus : public Node {
  public:
    Node *operand;
    Uminus( Node *o )
        : Node( UMINUS ), operand( o ) {}
};
```

```
class Int : public Node {
  public:
    int value;
    Int( int v )
        : Node( INT ), value( v ) {}
};
```

This arrangement is not too bad, although there is a lot of duplication between the two binary operators. As more binary operators are added to our calculator language this duplication becomes unwieldy and a potential source of errors. It is better to introduce another level of derivation that reflects their commonality.

```
class Binop : public Node {
  public:
    Node *left, *right;
    Binop( int c, Node *l, Node *r )
        : Node( c ), left( l ), right( r ) {}
};

class Plus : public Binop {
  public:
    Plus( Node *l, Node *r )
        : Binop( PLUS, l, r ) {}
};

class Times : public Binop {
  public:
    Times( Node *l, Node *r )
        : Binop( TIMES, l, r ) {}
};
```

The resulting hierarchy of class types shows how node types are related by inheritance.

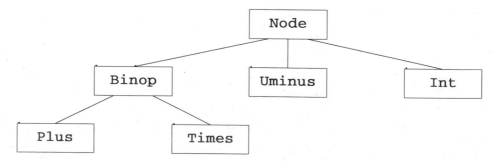

Thus a `Plus` is both a `Binop` and a `Node`, but not a `Uminus` or a `Times`. An `Int` is a `Node` but not a `Binop`, and so forth. If we have been careful in the design of our class hierarchy, these inheritance relationships between types should match our intuition about the concepts they represent in the problem domain. Inheritance is a conceptual aid as well as a method for code factoring and sharing.

```
int
Node::eval() const {
    switch( code ) {
    case INT:
        return ((Int *)this)->value;
    case UMINUS:
        return -((Uminus *)this)->operand->eval();
    case PLUS:
        return ((Binop *)this)->left->eval()
               + ((Binop *)this)->right->eval();
    case TIMES:
        return ((Binop *)this)->left->eval()
               * ((Binop *)this)->right->eval();
    default:
        error();
        return 0;
    }
}
```

Here we have implemented `Node::eval` by switching on `Node::code` and recursively evaluating subtrees. In order to call the correct `eval` member function, we have to cast the `this` pointer to the appropriate derived type object as indicated by the value of the node code. Since each class object of a type derived from `Node` is also a `Node`, a pointer to a `Node` is also a pointer to an object of the derived class indicated by `Node::code`. Casting the `this` pointer to the corresponding pointer to derived class type allows us to access the derived class members and perform the evaluation.

This is not too bad in this limited case, but it is easy to see how this approach could get out of hand in more complex situations, when one is forced to identify explicitly the correct `eval` routine before invocation.

Although our design works—we can build and evaluate abstract syntax trees—there is a major flaw in our implementation. We have implemented a hierarchy of node types, but in using an explicit node code, class `Node` essentially defines what node types can be derived from it.

The problem is obvious when we add a new type of node to the hierarchy. For example, if we want to add a divide operator, it is not sufficient simply to declare a class type derived from `Binop`. We must also change the implementation of `Node::eval` (and presumably add a new element to the enumeration of class `Node`). If the existing node hierarchy were part of a library, our users would be forced to copy and edit it to produce their own private version. In so doing, they would be putting themselves in the position of either tracking changes to the library in their private version or diverging from the standard library. In either case, our goal in providing a library will not have been met.

A better approach is to encapsulate node-specific information entirely within the appropriate node type without recording any node-specific information in node types higher up in the hierarchy. To do this effectively, we have to be able to distinguish between node types at runtime more effectively than we do in the current implementation of `Node::eval`, where we use a node code and explicit casts. We accomplish this with virtual functions.

5.4 Virtual Functions

Let us leave our abstract syntax tree example for a while and look at a simple example.

Suppose we are dealing with a collection of fruit types related by inheritance.

```
class Fruit {
  public:
    char *identify() { return "Fruit"; }
};

class Apple : public Fruit {
  public:
    char *identify() { return "Apple"; }
};

class Orange : public Fruit {
  public:
    char *identify() { return "Orange"; }
};
```

Our application is to create a heterogeneous list of fruit objects and have each list element identify itself. We use the singly linked list node type described earlier in this chapter.

```
typedef Fruit *Etype;
#include "listel.h"

void
print_list( ListEl *lst ) {
    extern void print( char * );
    while( lst ) {
        print( lst->value()->identify() );
        lst = lst->next();
    }
}

main() {
    ListEl *lst = new ListEl( new Fruit );
    lst = new ListEl( new Apple, lst );
    lst = new ListEl( new Orange, lst );
    print_list( lst );
}
```

This program prints the word "Fruit" three times even though the list contains an `Orange`, an `Apple`, and a `Fruit`. This behavior is to be expected because the expression `lst->value()` is of type `Fruit *`, and `Fruit::identify` returns a pointer to the character string "Fruit." Ordinarily the member function called depends on the type of the pointer or reference used to access it, not on the actual type of the object to which the pointer or reference refers. This is referred to as *static binding*, because the function to be called is determined when the program is compiled, rather than at runtime.

```
Fruit *fp = new Apple;
fp->identify(); // returns "Fruit"
((Apple *)fp)->identify();    // returns "Apple"
Apple *ap = (Apple *)fp;
ap->identify(); // returns "Apple"
```

Compare this to the implementation of `Node::eval` earlier in this chapter.

For our fruit identification program, however, we would like the proper identify function to be determined by the actual object type and not by the type of the pointer or reference used to access the object. For this we use virtual functions.

```
class Fruit {
  public:
    virtual char *identify() { return "Fruit"; }
};
```

Virtual functions allow derived classes to provide alternative versions for a base class function. In declaring `Fruit::identify` to be virtual, we are saying that classes derived from `Fruit` may have their own versions of `identify`, and that these functions should be invoked based on the actual object types. Thus an `Apple` or an `Orange` will have its own version of the virtual function invoked for it even when it is being treated as a generic `Fruit`. This is referred to as *dynamic binding*, since the precise version of the function called is determined at runtime rather than when the program is compiled.

Having added the keyword `virtual` to the declaration of `Fruit::identify`, our program now runs as we want it to, printing "Orange," "Apple," "Fruit."

Notice that `Apple::identify` and `Orange::identify` are virtual without our having explicitly declared them to be so (although we could have). The rules for determining when a function is virtual are simple: a function is virtual if it is declared virtual or if there is a base class function with the same signature that is virtual. A function's signature is composed of its name and its formal argument types. For example, if the declaration of `Apple::identify` were

```
char *identify( int = 0 );
```

then it would not be virtual, because it would then have a different signature from `Fruit::identify`. The output of our program in that case would be "Orange," "Fruit," "Fruit." If the signature of a derived class member function matches that of a base class virtual member, then the return type must also match that of the base class function. This ensures that the dynamic binding provided by virtual functions is type safe.

The combination of the is-a relationship from a derived class to its public base and dynamic binding of virtual functions is a useful abstraction method. For example, our `print_list` function deals only with lists of `Fruit` pointers. We can construct a hierarchy of types of arbitrary complexity and depth based on class `Fruit` without having to alter the implementation of

`print_list`. For example, we could widen the hierarchy by adding a
`Banana` type derived from `Fruit`, or extend the hierarchy downward by
deriving `Rome` and `Empire` from `Apple`. Inheritance used in this way allows us to abstract commonality from a group of related types and write general routines based on our abstraction. Type-specific details of derived types
are encapsulated within those types.

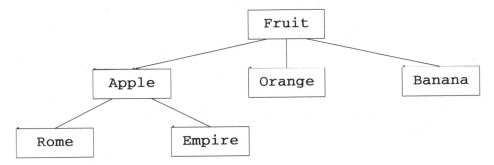

Using these concepts, we can now redesign our abstract syntax tree implementation to take advantage of virtual functions.

```
class Node {
  public:
    Node() {}
    virtual ~Node() {}
    virtual int eval() const { error(); return 0; }
};

class Binop : public Node {
  public:
    Node *left, *right;
    ~Binop() { delete left; delete right; }
    Binop( Node *l, Node *r ) : left( l ), right( r ) {}
};

class Plus : public Binop {
  public:
    Plus( Node *l, Node *r ) : Binop( l, r ) {}
    int eval() const
        { return left->eval() + right->eval(); }
};
```

```
class Times : public Binop {
  public:
    Times( Node *l, Node *r ) : Binop( l, r ) {}
    int eval() const
        { return left->eval() * right->eval(); }
};

class Uminus : public Node {
    Node *operand;
  public:
    Uminus( Node *o ) : operand( o ) {}
    ~Uminus() { delete operand; }
    int eval() const { return -operand->eval(); }
};

class Int : public Node {
    int value;
  public:
    Int( int v ) : value( v ) {}
    int eval() const { return value; }
};
```

In this implementation, eval is declared to be virtual in Node, so the evals in Plus, Times, Uminus, and Int are also virtual. Binop does not declare an eval function, so a Binop object would invoke Node::eval, inherited from its Node base class. Now we can create and evaluate abstract syntax trees.

```
int
limited_use() {
    // evaluate -11+21*93
    Node *np =
        new Plus(
            new Uminus(
                new Int( 11 )
            ),
            new Times(
                new Int( 21 ),
                new Int( 93 )
            )
        );
```

```
    int result = np->eval();
    delete np;
    return result;
}
```

The virtual call of `eval` invokes `Plus::eval` because a `Plus` node is at the root of the abstract syntax tree pointed to by `np`. `Plus::eval` invokes the virtual `eval` functions for its left and right subtrees, which in this case results in calls to `Uminus::eval` and `Times::eval`, respectively, and so on. At each step, the actual function invoked is determined by the type of the node at the root of the subtree being evaluated.

Class `Node` also declares a virtual destructor. The line

```
    delete np;
```

invokes the virtual destructor for the root of the abstract syntax tree pointed to by `np`. This is a `Plus` node, which defines no explicit destructor, so its base class's destructor, `Binop::~Binop`, does all the work. `Binop::~Binop` invokes the virtual destructors for its left and right subtrees, and so on. The result is that the single delete expression frees the entire abstract syntax tree.

As an aside, note that constructors cannot be virtual. A constructor creates an object, whereas a virtual function requires an already existing object to determine what function to call.

The use of virtual functions allows us to encapsulate node-specific operations within the declaration of a specific node type. We can now add new node types to the hierarchy without affecting existing code.

```
class Div : public Binop {
  public:
    Div( Node *l, Node *r ) : Binop( l, r ) {}
    int eval() const
        { return left->eval() / right->eval(); }
};
```

Having declared class `Div`, we can create and evaluate `Div` objects as nodes in an abstract syntax tree without changing the implementations of the other node types.

5.5 Designing for Inheritance

`Node::eval` serves a dual role. It is both the "root" virtual function that causes all the other `eval` members with the same signature to be virtual and a kind of stopgap. If we had forgotten to declare a `Div::eval`, any attempt to invoke `eval` for a `Div` node would result in a call to `Node::eval` and an error. No `Binop` or `Node` objects should be created or evaluated, only objects of classes derived from them. A stopgap function at the root of the hierarchy is an effective way of catching errors of this kind, but, unfortunately, the error is not evident until runtime, and only then if such a node is actually evaluated.

It is preferable (and safer) to prevent users of the node hierarchy from creating objects of these types at all. One way to do this is to make the constructors for `Node` and `Binop` private. Unfortunately, this will also prevent classes derived from them from using the constructors.

```
class Node {
    Node();
  public:
    // ...
};

class Int : public Node {
    int value;
  public:
    Int( int v ) : value( v ) {
        // error!  Implicit invocation of
        // private Node::Node
// ...
```

A similar problem arises with the members `left` and `right` of class `Binop`. We would prefer that they were private to protect them from abuse by casual users of the node hierarchy, but they must be public so that classes derived from `Binop` (`Plus`, `Times`, and `Div`) can use them.

We solve this problem with protected class members. A sequence of protected members is introduced in a class definition by a `protected` access specifier followed by a colon, just as public members can be introduced by `public` and private members by `private`. A protected member is similar to a private member in that it is not as accessible as a public member. However, it can be accessed by members and friends of classes derived from the class in which it is declared as well as by members and friends of the class in which it is declared. Similar to public members, a base class's protected members are protected in the derived class if the base is public, and private otherwise.

```
class Node {
  protected:
    Node() {}
  public:
    virtual ~Node() {}
    virtual int eval() const;
};

class Binop : public Node {
  protected:
    Node *left, *right;
    Binop( Node *l, Node *r ) : left( l ), right( r ) {}
    ~Binop() { delete left; delete right; }
};
```

Now only members and friends of `Node`, `Binop`, and classes derived from them can invoke their constructors; other code cannot allocate nodes of those types. Additionally, the `left` and `right` members of `Binop` can be accessed only by members and friends of binary operators derived from it.

The kind of protection provided by protected members differs from that provided by private members. Private members are class-oriented; they are accessible to members and friends of the class in which they are declared. Protected members are class-hierarchy-oriented. When we declare a member of a class to be protected, we are saying that the member is intended for use in objects of classes derived from that class. As we have seen, one of the purposes of class derivation is to customize the behavior of a base class; protected members represent an explicit interface for such customization. The difference arises in the following restriction: the friend or member function that has access to a protected member of a base class can only access that member through an object of that derived class or, by extension, through a class derived from that derived class.

Consider this restriction in the context of our abstract syntax tree hierarchy. A member or friend of `Plus` can access the `left` and `right` members of its `Binop` base class for any `Plus` object. This is appropriate, since (presumably) the members and friends of `Plus` know how `left` and `right` have been "customized" within a `Plus` object. However, it is illegal for a member or friend of `Plus` to access the `Binop::left` or

`Binop::right` of, say, a `Times` object, since `Times` may have "customized" these members differently.

As another example, consider augmenting the fruit hierarchy of this chapter to include a price.

```
class Fruit {
  protected:
    int price;
  public:
    void set_price( int p ) { price = p; }
    virtual void print_price() {}
    // ...
};
```

The `price` member really has no useful meaning, since it is not associated with a quantity or currency. The proper interpretation of the raw number is provided in each class derived from `Fruit`.

```
class Apple : public Fruit {
  public:
    void print_price()
       { printf( "%d cents (US) / bushel", price ); }
    // ...
};


class Banana : public Fruit {
  public:
    void print_price()
       { printf( "%d centimos (Costa Rica) / crate",
                   price ); }
    // ...
};
```

In this case, a member or friend of `Apple` could not be trusted to give the proper interpretation of `price` for a `Banana` object. Therefore, the members and friends of `Apple` have no special access privileges for the `price` protected member when it is accessed through a `Banana` object.

There are still problems with the the `Node` hierarchy. One problem has to do with safety. Even though `Node` and `Binop` have protected constructors, members and friends of these classes can still create objects of type `Node` and `Binop`. The second has to do with interface and implementation. The `eval` function of the `Node` base class must have an implementation even though no reasonable implementation exists. Additionally, it is not clear, when designing a derived class, whether or not one must override a given virtual function or whether it is permissible to inherit the base class version of the function. These problems are addressed by *pure virtual functions*.

A pure virtual function is indicated by appending the syntax `=  0;` to a function declaration in a class definition. For example, the `eval` member of class `Node` can be made pure.

```
class Node {
    // ...
    virtual int eval() const = 0;
    // ...
};
```

A pure virtual function need not have a definition. Any class containing a pure virtual function is called an *abstract base class*; the compiler will not permit an object of an abstract base class to be created, although pointers and references to abstract base classes may be. Any class derived from an abstract base class that does not override every pure virtual function inherited from the base is also abstract. For example, the `Node` class is abstract by virtue of its pure virtual `eval` function, and the `Binop` class is abstract because it inherits `eval` from `Node` without overriding it.

5.6   Inheritance as a Design Tool

Inheritance is a design method in that it allows one to abstract a problem to its most general form in a base class at the root of a hierarchy, and model and write code dealing only with the abstraction. Specialized cases (which may themselves be abstractions of even more specialized cases) can then be handled with classes derived from the base class.

For example, in the abstract syntax tree example we started with a general concept of node and successively expanded the node type hierarchy by specialization. However, the original abstraction remains. In code like

```
void
print_value( Node *np ) {
    extern void print( int );
    print( np->eval() );
}
```

we are dealing only with Nodes, and the complexities of the specialized types derived from Node remain hidden from general-purpose routines.

As a design tool, the use of inheritance is similar to that of stepwise refinement of the function decomposition paradigm described in Chapter 2. Stepwise refinement divides the procedural aspects of a problem into a hierarchy of procedures, whereas inheritance divides the type aspects of a problem into a hierarchy of types.

Although the result of developing a program by stepwise refinement is a strict hierarchy of procedures, one does not necessarily arrive at that result in a strictly top-down fashion. Sometimes low-level procedures are coded first to see how their implementation affects the structure of procedures higher in the hierarchy.

In a similar way, in a complex program that deals with many different types it may not be obvious how the types are related to each other, if at all. Sometimes it is only after having coded the implementations of several seemingly disparate types that their commonality is evident. Inheritance can then be used to share the common parts of their interface and implementation. Frequently, this commonality is evidence of a deeper abstraction, and the "discovered" inheritance hierarchy becomes a working design abstraction.

Consider as a meta-example the implementation of a symbol table for a C++ compiler. In the interest of brevity we will simplify a bit, but the general framework of the solution could be (and has been) used to develop a symbol table for a C++ compiler.

Let us review the basics of scope in C++. Scope in C++ is essentially block-structured. That is, a name is defined from its point of first appearance to the end of the block in which it is defined. The appearance of a name in an inner block hides all names with the same identifier defined in outer blocks. For the purpose of symbol management, the file itself can be considered to be a block.

Member functions and inheritance increase the complexity of this simple block structure. The enclosing scope of a member function is the scope of the class of which it is a member.

```
    int i;
    class C {
        int i;
        void f() { i = 1; }
    };
```

The member function f assigns to the class member i, not the global i. The following fragment is equivalent to the previous one:

```
    int i;
    class C {
        int i;
        void f();
    };
    void C::f() { i = 1; }
```

The enclosing scope of a member function is its class whether or not it is textually enclosed within the class.

The enclosing scope of a derived class is its base class. For example:

```
    class B { public: int i; };
    int i;
    void g() {
        static int i;
        class D1 : public B {
            void f() { i = 1; }
        };
    }
    class D2 : public B {};
```

Classes B, D1, and D2 form a class hierarchy in which B is the enclosing scope for both D1 and D2. In particular, note that the immediate enclosing scope for D1 is not the scope of the function g, but the base class B, followed by g. Thus the member function f of D1 assigns to the base class member i, not the local or file scope i.

As a first approach to the design of the symbol table, we decide to represent the various flavors of scope (global, class, function) as separate tables rather than maintain a single monolithic structure. We represent each kind of table as a separate class with member functions for lookup and insertion of names.

```
class Name;

class Gtab {
  public:
    Name *insert( const char * );
    Name *lookup( const char * ) const;
};

class Ftab {
  public:
    Name *insert( const char * );
    Name *lookup( const char * ) const;
};
```

In addition, because the scope of a derived class is nested within that of its base class, the class table type has a member that refers to its base class's table. This is used by `Ctab::lookup` to search its base classes' tables.

```
class Ctab {
    const Ctab *base_class;
  public:
    Name *insert( const char * );
    Name *lookup( const char * ) const;
};
```

In each case, the argument to the insertion or lookup function is a pointer to an identifier, and the return value is a symbol table name. For purposes of this illustration, we consider a `Name` to be an object containing an identifier and possibly other information.

Having partitioned our problem into three separate cases, we are free to implement each table's abstract semantics in whatever way is most appropriate to each case. For instance, we may have developed a heuristic that indicates a class table is best organized as a list, the global table as a simple hash table, and a function table as a more complex hash table that keeps track of block scope within the function. The single global table might be structured as follows:

```
class Gtab {
    enum { TSZ = 256 };
    static Name *t[ TSZ ];
    static int hash( const char * );
  public:
    Name *insert( const char * );
    Name *lookup( const char * ) const;
} gtable;
```

At this point, we have a complete representation for a given scope. We maintain the stack of currently open, nested scopes in a list.

```
struct Scope {
    enum { FUNC, CLASS, GLOBAL } type;
    union {
    Ftab *fptr;
    Ctab *cptr;
    Gtab *gptr;
    };
};
List<Scope> scope_list;
```

However, although this approach will work, it makes the code for simple insertions and lookups rather complex.

```
Name *
lookup( const char *id ) {
    Name *n;
    for( ListCtl<Scope> i = scope_list; i; i.next() ) {
        const Scope * const s = i.get();
        switch( s->type ) {
        case Scope::FUNC:
            if( n = s->fptr->lookup( id ) )
                return n;
            break;
        case Scope::CLASS:
            if( n = s->cptr->lookup( id ) )
                return n;
            break;
```

```
        case Scope::GLOBAL:
            if( n = s->gptr->lookup( id ) )
                return n;
            break;
        }
    }
    return 0;
}


Name *
insert( const char *id ) {
    const Scope * const curr = scope_list.head();
    if( curr )
        switch( curr->type ) {
        case Scope::FUNC:
            return curr->fptr->insert( id )
        case Scope::CLASS:
            return curr->cptr->insert( id );
        case Scope::GLOBAL:
            return curr->gptr->insert( id );
        }
    return 0;
}
```

Under this scheme, we must always distinguish between specific types of
scope even in situations where we are performing generic operations.

An alternate approach is to recognize the commonality of these three
symbol table types and use inheritance to make the commonality explicit. In
essence, we are "factoring out" their commonality into a base class.

```
class Tab {
  protected:
    static Tab *curr_tab;  // current active scope
    Tab *parent;     // enclosing scope
  public:
    static Name *find( const char * );
    static Name *enter( const char * );
    virtual Name *insert( const char * ) = 0;
    virtual Name *lookup( const char * ) const = 0;
    // ...
};
```

```
class Gtab : public Tab { /* ... */ };
class Ctab : public Tab { /* ... */ };
class Ftab : public Tab { /* ... */ };
```

Here we represent the enclosing scope explicitly as a pointer to the `Tab` type at the root of the symbol table hierarchy. Since `Tab` is a public base class of `Gtab`, `Ctab`, and `Ftab`, `Tab::parent` can refer to any symbol table object. To keep track of the current scope, we use a static class variable of type `Tab *`, `curr_tab`, to point to the current table.

Now we have a workable framework for our C++ symbol table. At any given time the state of scope consists of the ensemble of the individual function and class tables, and the global table. The relationships among these tables are represented by their parent pointers and, in the case of class tables, by their base class pointers.

When a new scope comes into existence, say at the beginning of a class body, we create a new class table and initialize it to refer to the proper enclosing scope and base class. For instance, if the class is a derived class, it occurs in the scope of its base class, so its `base_class` pointer is set to the table of its base class. Its `parent` pointer is set to the table representing its enclosing class or function, or to the global scope. Rewritten to take advantage of the table hierarchy and virtual functions it makes possible, the general lookup and insertion routines become noticeably simpler. We also take advantage of the existence of a generic symbol table type to encapsulate the interface better by making these generic operations static members of the `Tab` class.

```
Name *
Tab::find( const char *id ) {
    Name *n;
    for( Tab *t = curr_tab; t; t = t->parent )
        if( n = t->lookup( id ) )
            return n;
    return 0;
}

Name *
Tab::enter( const char *id ) {
    { return curr_tab->insert( id ); }
```

Having expressed the relationship of our three original symbol table types as special cases of a general table type, we have not only simplified use of the types but, in developing an abstraction of a symbol table, we have simplified the way we *think* about the types.

5.7 Inheritance for Interface Sharing

In some of the examples in this chapter, derived classes are augmentations or specializations of base classes that are fully usable types in their own right. `List2El` is derived from `ListEl`, and `Pathname` from `String`, but both `ListEl` and `String` are perfectly functional types. On the other hand, the base `Tab` type of our symbol table hierarchy and `Node` of our abstract syntax tree node hierarchy are not fully functional and require that their definition be completed by class derivation. In a sense, `Tab` and `Node` are partial types, half implementation and half template, that are completed in classes derived from them.

We can extend this concept, and define a base class that is intended strictly as an interface description for classes derived from it, in order to guarantee that a derived type satisfies a certain interface. Here we would regard a derived class not as an augmentation or specialization of its base class but rather as a realization of the interface specified by its base class.

Consider the task of specifying the interface between the kernel and a device driver in an operating system. To issue a call to open, close, read, write, and so on, a given device, we have decided to implement the interface as a class type that encapsulates the behavior of a generic device driver.

```
class Device {
  protected:
    Device();
  public:
    virtual ~Device();
    virtual int open( char *, int, int );
    virtual int close( int );
    virtual int read( int, char *, unsigned ) = 0;
    virtual int write( int, char *, unsigned ) = 0;
    virtual int ioctl( int, int ... ) = 0;
};
```

These generic device driver member functions implement default behavior

```
int
Device::open( char *path, int oflag, int mode )
   { return nulldev(); }
```

or specify that there is no reasonable default by declaring the operation to be a pure virtual function.

Now the kernel can deal with all devices through this generic device type just as we earlier evaluated all abstract syntax tree node types through a generic `Node` type, and accessed all symbol tables through a generic `Tab` type.

We create a type for a specific kind of device driver by derivation from this abstract base class.

```
class Terminal : public Device {
  public:
    Terminal();
    ~Terminal();
    int open( char *, int, int );
    int close( int );
    int read( int, char *, unsigned );
    int write( int, char *, unsigned );
    int ioctl( int, int ... );
};
```

Any part of the interface not explicitly redefined in the derived device type defaults to the routine in the base type.

```
class MemMappedIo : public Device {
  public:
    int read( int, char *, unsigned );
    int write( int, char *, unsigned );
    int ioctl( int, int ... );
};
```

The `MemMappedIo` device type only supplies definitions of the pure virtual functions, which is the minimum required for `MemMappedIo` objects to be created. It inherits from `Device` the other member function, including the virtual functions with default implementations, and allows the compiler to generate a default constructor and destructor for it.

5.8 Multiple Inheritance

A derived class can have any number of base classes. The use of two or more base classes is called multiple inheritance. Although the uses of multiple inheritance appear to be less common than those of single inheritance, multiple inheritance is useful for creating class types that combine the properties of two or more other class types.

For example, we may want to create a type that monitors a given condition and displays its status on the screen. Suppose we have a bit-map graphics library available with a dial abstract data type that displays a changing value.

```cpp
class Dial {
  public:
    Dial( const char *label, double low, double high );
    ~Dial();
    void set_display_value( double );
  private:
    // ...
};
```

The `Dial` constructor displays a dial with the argument label, and with measurement range between the values of the second and third arguments. After creation, a `Dial` object continuously displays the last value sent as as argument to `Dial::set_display_value`.

We also have available a sampler type.

```cpp
class Sampler {
  protected:
    Sampler( double frequency );
    virtual void sample() = 0;
  public:
    virtual ~Sampler();
  private:
    // ...
};
```

A `Sampler` object simply invokes its virtual `sample` function every `frequency` seconds, where `frequency` is the argument to the `Sampler` constructor.

Our monitor type is both a `Dial` and a `Sampler`. We express this by using multiple inheritance to inherit from both classes.

```
class Monitor : public Sampler, public Dial {
    void sample();
  protected:
    Monitor( char *lab, double l, double h, double f )
        : Dial( lab, l, h ), Sampler( f ) {}
    virtual double get_display_value() = 0;
};
```

The syntax

```
class Monitor : public Sampler, public Dial
```

declares `Monitor` to be a new class type derived from both `Dial` and `Sampler`. The use of multiple base classes is a natural extension of the single inheritance case of a single base class. Any number of class names can be present on the comma-separated base class list, but no name can appear twice on the same list.

The `Monitor` constructor uses a member initialization list to invoke the base class constructors explicitly. The base classes are initialized in the order they appear in the class definition, without regard for the order the initializations appear in the member initialization list. Recall that base classes are always initialized before members even if a member name occurs before a base class name on a member initialization list.

The scope of class `Monitor` "nests" within the scopes of *both* its base classes. Therefore, `Monitor::sample` is a virtual function that overrides the base class pure virtual `Sampler::sample`. The reference to `set_display_value` in `Monitor::sample` refers to `Dial::set_display_value`. The implementation of `Monitor::sample` serves to connect the sampler service provided by `Sampler` with the display service provided by `Dial`.

```
void
Monitor::sample()
    { set_display_value( get_display_value() ); }
```

The function invokes the pure virtual `get_display_value` and sends the returned value to the non-virtual `set_display_value` function inherited from `Dial`.

The "multiple nesting" engendered by multiple inheritance can be a source of ambiguities that do not occur under single inheritance. To illustrate some of these problems, let us return to our hierarchy of fruit types and also include a hierarchy of tree types.

```
class Fruit {
  public:
    virtual char *identify() { return "Fruit"; }
};

class Tree {
  public:
    virtual char *identify() { return "Tree"; }
};
```

Some types are both `Fruit` and `Tree`.

```
class Apple : public Fruit, public Tree {};

Apple *ap = new Apple;
ap->identify(); // error!
```

The code does not compile because the function call is ambiguous. Since the scope of `Apple` nests in the scopes of both `Fruit` and `Tree`, the call could refer to either `Fruit::identify` or `Tree::identify`. We can make the call unambiguous by being explicit about the base class to which we refer, either by using the scope operator

```
ap->Fruit::identify();
```

or a cast:

```
((Fruit *)ap)->identify();
```

A better solution is to define an `identify` function for class `Apple` with the desired behavior. This function will override both `Fruit::identify` and `Tree::identify`.

```
class Apple : public Fruit, public Tree {
  public:
    char *identify() { return "Apple"; }
};
// ...
ap->identify(); // unambiguous
```

All the usual relationships hold between a derived class and each of its base classes under multiple inheritance as they would with a single base class. For instance, `Apple::identify` is a virtual function that redefines both `Tree::identify` and `Fruit::identify`. Additionally, because both `Fruit` and `Tree` are public base classes of `Apple`, there are predefined conversions from `Apple` to both `Fruit` and `Tree`.

```
Apple a;
Tree &t = a; // OK, an Apple is-a Tree
Fruit *f = &a;  // OK, an Apple is-a Fruit
*f = t;         // error! a Tree is not a Fruit
a = t;     // error! a Fruit is not an Apple
```

Compare the above to the conversions described earlier for the abstract syntax tree node hierarchy.

Let us return to our `Monitor` class. Using multiple inheritance we have combined two separate services, a `Dial` and a `Sampler`, to produce a new type. This use of multiple inheritance for combining types is a very important one.

Now we can derive specialized monitor types from class `Monitor`. A type derived from `Monitor` has to provide initializing values to be passed through the `Monitor` constructor to the `Dial` and `Sampler` constructors as well as override the pure virtual `Monitor::get_display_value` function that provides the value to be monitored.

```
class MemUsage : public Monitor {
   char *start;
   char *max;
 public:
   double get_display_value()
       { return (current_top()-start)/(max-start); }
   MemUsage() : Monitor( "Memory Usage", 0, 100, 0.1 ),
       start( current_top() ), max( get_limit() ) {}
};
```

A `MemUsage` object monitors the percent of available memory in use by the process in which it occurs. The virtual `get_display_value` function returns the fraction of available memory used since the `MemUsage` object was created. A system function, here called `current_top`, provides the top memory address of the process for the calculation. The constructor labels the monitor dial "Memory Usage," sets the displayed range of values between `0.0` and `100.0`, and sets the sampling rate to ten times per second. Note that `current_top` is used again to record the starting top memory address of the process. Another system function, called `get_limit`, provides the maximum address to which the process memory is allowed to grow.

Like operator overloading, multiple inheritance is a feature that is often subject to abuse by overuse. For instance, the `Monitor` type could have been implemented with single inheritance, by layering a `Dial` as a member and inheriting from `Sampler`. However, the is-a relationship would then no longer hold between a `Monitor` and a `Dial`. If such a relationship is important to understanding the abstract design, or if the automatic conversions that accompany an is-a relationship are frequently used (a `Monitor` is frequently used as a `Dial`) then the use of multiple inheritance is appropriate. Otherwise, the simpler use of single inheritance is preferable.

The most common proper use of multiple inheritance is for a class that is part of a "natural" single inheritance hierarchy to employ multiple inheritance to additionally inherit one or more interfaces.

For example, the single inheritance version of the `Monitor` type described above may have to respond to a protocol established by a controller subsystem. The protocol can be encapsulated in a class.

```
class Protocol {
  protected:
    Protocol();
  public:
    virtual ~Protocol();
    virtual void activate() = 0;
    virtual void deActivate() = 0;
    virtual void reSync() = 0;
};
```

The controller subsystem can deal with `Protocol` objects only, so the `Monitor` type has to be (also) a `Protocol`; there must be an is-a relationship between `Monitor` and `Protocol`.

```
class Monitor : public Sampler, public Protocol {
  // ...
  void activate();
  void deActivate();
  void reSync();
  // ...
};
```

The `Monitor` overrides the pure virtual functions in the `Protocol` interface specification so it will respond in the correct, `Monitor`-specific way to messages from the controller subsystem. The controller subsystem deals with the `Protocol` class and need not be aware of the existence of objects of types derived from it.

5.9 Virtual Base Classes

The `Monitor` type uses multiple inheritance to combine two entirely distinct classes. Multiple inheritance can also be used to combine more closely related classes. For example, we might want to create a new device type that has properties from two existing device types.

```
class MonitoredDevice :
    public Device, public Monitor {
    // ...
};

class NetworkDevice :
    public Device, public Protocol {
    // ...
};
```

A `MonitoredDevice` monitors the transmission rate of data through a device, and a `NetworkDevice` is an interface to a network driver board that obeys a given network protocol. We would like to create a new device type that monitors a network transmission rate. We could construct a new device type "from scratch,"

```
class MonitoredNetworkDevice :
    public Device, public Monitor, public Protocol {
    // ...
};
```

but we would not be able to use our new type as a `NetworkDevice` or a `MonitoredDevice` because there would then be no inheritance relation between the types.

The alternative of deriving from the two existing devices would cause two `Device` base classes to appear in the hierarchy.

```
class MonitoredNetworkDevice :
    public MonitoredDevice, public NetworkDevice {
    // ...
};
```

In some cases, this is just what is required, but it is not what we need for our new device type. First, any simple attempt to use the new type as a device would result in ambiguity errors, and we would always have to specify the instance of `Device` to which we were referring.

```
MonitoredNetworkDevice iso;
iso.open( "/dev/iso", O_RDWR, 0 );
          // error! ambiguous
iso.Device::open( "/dev/iso", O_RDWR, 0 );
          // error! still ambiguous
iso.NetworkDevice::open( "/dev/iso", O_RDWR, 0 );
          // OK, NetworkDevice's Device
iso.MonitoredDevice::open( "/dev/iso", O_RDWR, 0 );
          // OK, MonitoredDevice's Device
```

A more basic problem is that, although we are dealing with a single physical device, our type contains two separate representations of it. This is bound to cause difficulties. For instance, because the `Device` constructor would be activated twice for each `MonitoredNetworkDevice` object, the operating system kernel, which deals with devices entirely through the interface provided by the `Device` type, would probably conclude that there are two devices where there is only one.

What we would like to do is create a class that is derived from both `MonitoredDevice` and `NetworkDevice` but that has only a single instance of `Device`. We accomplish this with virtual base classes.

```
class MonitoredDevice :
   public virtual Device, public Monitor {
   // ...
};

class NetworkDevice :
   public virtual Device, public Protocol {
   // ...
};

class MonitoredNetworkDevice :
   public MonitoredDevice, public NetworkDevice {
   // ...
};
```

In declaring a base class virtual we are saying that we want its representation to be shared with every other virtual occurrence of that base class in an object. There is only a single occurrence of `Device` in the class

`MonitoredNetworkDevice`, because both occurrences of `Device` are declared to be virtual. Since there is only a single `Device`, unqualified references to its members are no longer ambiguous.

```
iso.open( "/dev/iso", O_RDWR, 0 );  // unambiguous
```

Likewise, the `Device` constructor is invoked only once for a `MonitoredNetworkDevice` object, because there is only one `Device` to initialize.

There are some subtleties associated with the use of virtual base classes. Any initialization of virtual base classes is done before any other base class, and the initialization is always accomplished by the appropriate constructor in the *most derived class*, that is, the class of the entire object, and not one of its base class *sub-object*s. In our example, the `Device` virtual base class in a `MonitoredNetworkDevice` object is initialized by a `MonitoredNetworkDevice` constructor, and not by `NetworkDevice` or `MonitoredDevice` constructor. In a `NetworkDevice` object, of course, the initialization would be accomplished by a `NetworkDevice` constructor.

5.10 Exercises

Exercise 5-1. Why do we call `ListEl` a list element class rather than a list class? □

Exercise 5-2. Consider each of the following problem domains: bank accounts, derivative securities, online documentation, data structures used for containment, sorting algorithms, zoo animals, tokens returned by a lexical analyser, GUI interface protocols, employee database records. Develop hierarchies for each that reflects your abstract notion of how each domain is structured, and decide what operations should be associated with each level of abstraction. Code your hierarchy in C++ using class derivation, non-virtual, virtual, and pure virtual functions as appropriate. □

Exercise 5-3. Consider the graph and finite state automaton abstract data types from the exercises of the previous chapter. Can one be derived from the other? Can they share a common base class? How would you characterize each of these uses of inheritance: as code sharing only, or is there a conceptual commonality between graphs and finite state automata? □

Exercise 5-4. †Add identifier and assignment node types to the calculator abstract syntax tree node hierarchy. Do you have to change the implementation of the other node types to do this? Use the resulting node hierarchy to write a complete interactive calculator program. □

Exercise 5-5. In the implementation of `operator +` (concatenation) for the `Pathname` type, what would happen if we did not cast the first `Pathname&` argument to `String&`? □

Exercise 5-6. Implement the `Pathname` type using `String` as a member rather than as a base class. What differences in behavior will the two implementations of `Pathname` exhibit? If inheritance in this case is used solely to obtain an automatic conversion from a `Pathname` to a `String`, would the use of a conversion operator, in lieu of inheritance, be more appropriate? □

Exercise 5-7. Assume the existence of a hardware interface library for terminal devices with the following inheritance hierarchy:

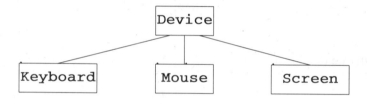

Suppose you could not modify the library and had to add tablet and light pen types into the hierarchy. Where and how would you add them? Suppose you could modify the library. How would you add the types now? How would you restructure the hierarchy to ease the introduction of new types in the future? □

Exercise 5-8. †Modify the implementation of the generic list-of-pointers class of Exercise 4-10 so that an unbounded number of new list types can be instantiated without causing any additional code to be generated. □

Exercise 5-9. Show how inheritance can be used to package and supply a set of constants to other class types. □

Exercise 5-10. Use the `Monitor` type to create class types that monitor a) typing speed, b) the number of users logged on to the system, †d) number of abstract syntax tree nodes allocated, and d) relative percentage of binary operator nodes to unary operator nodes. □

Exercise 5-11. Rewrite the `Monitor` type without the use of multiple inheritance. What are the relative advantages of each implementation? Are the two implementations equivalent, or do they exhibit different behavior? □

Exercise 5-12. Consider the following protocol class.

```
class OnOff {
  protected:
   OnOff();
  public:
   virtual ~OnOff() {}
   virtual void turnOn() = 0;
   virtual void turnOff() = 0;
};
```

Use multiple inheritance to add the `OnOff` protocol to the single inheritance version of the `Monitor` of the previous exercise. Derive a new monitor class and test its response to the protocol with the following driver.

```
void
controller( OnOff &thing ) {
    while( 1 ) {
        char buf[ 81 ];
        cin >> buf;
        if( strcmp( buf, "off" ) == 0 )
            thing.turnOff();
        else if( strcmp( buf, "on" ) == 0 )
            thing.turnOn();
    }
}
```

□

Exercise 5-13. Show how inheritance can be used to provide different "views" of a given base class. Design a database record for an employee database and supply derived class views appropriate for a) general use, b) payroll, c) supervision, and d) the FBI. □

Exercise 5-14. Write access abstractions for the employee database record that accomplish the same ends as the inheritance hierarchy of the previous exercise. What are the advantages and disadvantages of each approach? □

Exercise 5-15. Use `sizeof` to find the number of bytes objects of each of the following classes occupies.

```
class C1 { int i; };
class C2 { int i; void f(); };
class C3 { int i; virtual void f(); };
class C4 { int i; virtual void f1(); virtual void f2(); };
```

What do your results allow you to hypothesize about the implementation of non-virtual member and virtual member functions by your C++ compiler? □

Exercise 5-16. Use `sizeof` to find the number of bytes that each of the following classes occupies.

```
class V1 { int i; };
class V2 { int i; };
class C1 : virtual public V1 { int i; };
class C2 : virtual public V1, virtual public V2 { int i; };
```

What do your results allow you to hypothesize about the implementation of virtual base classes by your C++ compiler? □

Exercise 5-17. Design a type that monitors the price of a stock, issuing buy and sell transactions as appropriate. □

Exercise 5-18. †If it were legal to declare a virtual constructor, what would its meaning be? Devise a technique to implement your concept of a virtual constructor. □

Exercise 5-19. Use your solution to the previous exercise as the basis for implementing a "dup" member function for the `Node` hierarchy of this chapter. Invoking "dup" on a given node in an abstract syntax tree will return a pointer to an exact copy of the subtree rooted at that node. □

Exercise 5-20. A persistent object is an object that can be translated, correctly, to a different address space. For example, an object that can be written to secondary storage and later read back into a different memory location, or an object that can be transmitted across a network, is persistent. Some of the more difficult problems of implementing a general persistence mechanism for class objects arise because of inheritance. These problems include the necessity of restoring a derived class that is referred to by a base class pointer and restoring the internal mechanisms that implement a class object's virtual functions and virtual base classes.

Outline a design of a general persistence mechanism. Consider the use of any or all of virtual constructors, virtual base classes, and copy constructors in your approach. □

Exercise 5-21. Add flow-of-control constructs to the calculator abstract syntax trees of this chapter. Design a class that allows you to create and modify abstract syntax trees and provides a way to execute the resultant trees. Design a calculator language with a concrete syntax to match that of the abstract syntax trees, and write a constructor that will produce an abstract syntax tree object from a character string containing the concrete syntax.

Based on your experience, outline the design of Lisp and Smalltalk classes that encapsulate interpreters for Lisp and Smalltalk which can be invoked from C++ programs. Based on your experience, outline the design of a C++ interpreter that can be invoked from C++ programs. □

Exercise 5-22. †Explain why class-scoped enumerator `TSZ` was used instead of a constant or literal in the implementation of the `Gtab` class of this chapter. □

CHAPTER 6: **Object-Oriented Programming**

Procedural programming techniques focus on the algorithms used to solve a problem, leaving the data structures that are acted on by functions as separate parts of the program organization. In contrast, object-oriented programming focuses on the domain of the problem for which the program is written; the elements of the program design correspond to objects in the problem description. The general approach of object-oriented programming is to define a collection of object types. Object types are modules that integrate the data structures that represent the elements of the problem with the operations needed to produce a solution. Once these object types are defined, instances of objects for the specific problem are created, and operations are invoked to do the processing.

In C++, classes serve as object types, and member functions provide the means for building operations into the type.

6.1 Designing Objects

Object-oriented program design is an extension of the use of data abstraction. The abstract data types, or object types, not only hide the structure of data but encapsulate all the processing as operations on objects. The essence of object-oriented design is to find the most suitable object types for a specific programming problem. When a program is representative of others in the same field, a goal of object-oriented design is to find the objects suitable not only for use in the solution to the immediate problem, but also for reuse in other programs in the same domain.

Judging and comparing the suitability of designs can be difficult. General goals for a program design include efficiency and maintainability as well as correctness. Exact program requirements and design trade-offs are usually not completely understood without experimentation. Design for reuse is even harder to judge, since the characteristics of a specific problem must be generalized, and the needs of future programs must be anticipated. A reusable design also must be easily understood by programmers who were not the original designers.

Some design principles are well enough understood that there are useful heuristics to follow, although general rules should be applied with care since large programs often have complicated characteristics that make the design problem practically unique. Qualities of a design that have practical consequences in program efficiency, maintainability, and component reusability are described in aesthetic terms like elegance, simplicity, and consistency. Good software design depends on common sense and aesthetic sense, although tools and techniques can provide considerable help in structuring the problem and a solution.

Before discussing some guidelines for designing object types, let us look at two object-oriented programs that sort a list of integers. To focus on the design, we will not show the details of the implementations. The first program uses an `Intlist` abstract data type that contains operators to sort and output the list. Integers are read into the list when an `Intlist` object is created.

```
class Intlist {
    // etc.
  public:
    Intlist();
    sort();
    write();
};

main() {
    Intlist *ilist = new Intlist();
    ilist->sort();
    ilist->write();
}
```

The other program uses a `Sortedintlist` abstract data type, which reads in integers in the process of creating a sorted list. `Sortedintlist` contains an operator for output.

```
class Sortedintlist {
    // etc.
  public:
    Sortedintlist();
    write();
};

main() {
    Sortedintlist *slist = new Sortedintlist();
    slist->write();
}
```

Which of these has the better design, or are they equally good?

A good guideline for designing object types is to look for nouns and verbs in the description of the problem to be solved. The nouns become objects in the program design, and the verbs become the operations. Using this rule on the problem, ''Sort a list of integers,'' the program design should include a ''list of integers'' object type that has a ''sort'' operation. The `Intlist` program more closely matches the ''natural'' solution suggested by the problem description, whereas the second program invents a specialized type not clearly necessary for the solution. The added specialization and implementation overhead of sorting the list on creation may be inappropriate for use in another program that requires only the general storage mechanism of a simple list.

A sorted list type might be just the type for different problems, especially as a case of a more general list. For example, in a program that performs a wide variety of list processing, a sorted list type might be useful to optimize searching or merging of lists. A compressed list type, representing lists with no duplicate elements, could also be part of a general list processing program.

This brings out another aspect of object-oriented design: the use of inheritance to create specialized versions of basic object types. Rather than create an entirely different object type for each application, one builds new types from general base types. In our hypothetical list processing program, we would use `List` as our base class and have `Sortedlist` and `Compressedlist` as classes derived from `List`. The `sort` operation could be declared as a virtual function in the base class. The version of `sort` in `Sortedlist` would do nothing. No special version of `sort` would be needed for `Compressedlist`.

The inheritance relation between a base class and a specialized derived class is known as the *is-a* relation in object-oriented design jargon. A

`Sortedlist` is a `List` in that it has the same operations and can be used anywhere that a `List` is called for. Inheritance separates the general characteristics of the base class from specialized behavior in derived classes. Code that is written for base class objects can be used on all derived class objects.

A guideline for recognizing when inheritance might be used for type specialization in an object-oriented design is to look for adjectives in the programming problem description. For the list processing problem, ''sorted list'' and ''compressed list'' indicate when derived types could be used.

Another aspect of object-oriented design is recognizing a generic type. Again, in the list processing program, there might be ''lists of integers,'' ''lists of strings,'' and ''lists of employee records.'' All these lists of different element types could be built as instantiations of a generic list type. A clue for recognizing a generic type is that it is a container for other types and has no other function than to organize what it contains. It is probably not worthwhile building a generic type, however, unless a program uses more than one instance of the type, or the type is to be reused in other programs.

6.2 Finding Objects

A problem description does not always conveniently identify the most appropriate object types with which to implement a program. Finding an abstraction common to a number of objects so that they can share one base type implementation is not necessarily a straightforward task. Designing a program is often a trial and error process, requiring several attempts at a precise problem description, identification of abstractions, and prototype implementations. This is not new or peculiar to object-oriented design.

What is new in object-oriented programming is the way of thinking of programs as implementations of object types instead of as implementations of algorithms. This conceptual shift is sometimes hard for a programmer to make. Abstract concepts and entities that are not tangible things may be particularly hard to recognize as candidates for object types.

It is not difficult to conceive of object types that correspond to real-world physical objects with which we are familiar. For example, devices like disk and tape drives are physical objects. A device is one of the object types in the domain of an operating system kernel. In Chapter 5, we presented a class to serve as a generic interface to device drivers.

```
class Device {
  protected:
    Device();
  public:
    virtual ~Device();
    virtual int open( char *, int, int );
    virtual int close( int );
    virtual int read( int, char *, unsigned ) = 0;
    virtual int write( int, char *, unsigned ) = 0;
    virtual int ioctl( int, int ... ) = 0;
};
```

This class can also be thought of as the base object type for all varieties of devices in an object-oriented design of an operating system. Using inheritance, variations of the type can be created to represent disk devices and tape devices.

```
class Disk : public Device {
  public:
    int open( char *, int, int );
    int close( int );
    int read( int, char *, unsigned );
    int write( int, char *, unsigned );
    int ioctl( int, int ... );
    Disk();
    ~Disk();
};

class Tape : public Device {
  public:
    // etc.
};
```

Although there are a variety of different device types, the kernel's view is of a number of similar device objects.

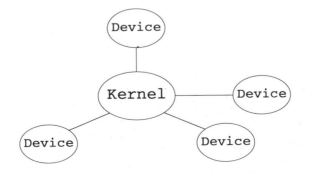

Many programs never deal directly with intuitively understandable representations of physical objects. The object types needed in these cases are part of an abstract problem domain. In an operating system, a process could be an object even though ''process'' is conceived of as an activity.

A typical operating system kernel might represent a process by scattered data structures and functions that manipulate the various structures. In an object-oriented design, these data structures and functions are packed together in a class to create a process object type. The interface to the object type is the set of functions by which the kernel controls processes. In our example below, `class Proc` provides functions to put a process to sleep waiting for a certain event at a certain priority, to wake up a sleeping process, to save and restore the state of a running process, and to send a message, in the form of a message number, to the process. A copy constructor is provided so that a new `Proc` can be created from another, as when processes are forked. The destructor removes a terminated process from the system. Operations for swapping a processes in and out of the system are not provided in the example interface because these are considered part of the memory management of the hidden elements of the `Proc` object.

```
class Proc {
  public:
    int sleep( Sleepq *, int  );
    void wakeup();
    int save_runstate();
    void resume_runstate();
    int send_msg( int );
    Proc( Proc & );
    ~Proc();
};
```

Process objects can now be added to the kernel's view of its domain:

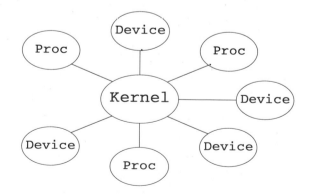

To continue our system design to include the kernel, a decision must be made on the nature of the relationship between the kernel and device or process objects. Are devices and processes component parts of the kernel, or are they independent entities on which the kernel invokes operations? The choice is between what are known as the *has-a* and *uses-a* relationships in object-oriented design jargon. If it is decided that there is a kernel object that has devices and processes as parts, the class implementing the kernel will have data members that represent these parts. If it is decided that the kernel only uses device and process objects by invoking actions on them, it is possible for the kernel to have either an object-oriented or procedural design. C++ allows a hybrid program design, and objects can by manipulated by non-member functions as well as by other objects. Objects are powerful abstractions that can simplify a complicated program design, but procedural abstractions have also been used successfully in solving certain kinds of programming problems, including the design of central control functions for an operating system.

Further analysis is required to address the kernel design issues. The presumption that the kernel is a single design element was a simplification used to focus considerations on devices and processes. The desired functionality of the kernel needs to be explored and further decomposed, either by identifying more objects, or, if deemed appropriate, by using procedural techniques. Additional candidates for consideration as objects in the kernel design are entities such as state, interrupt, buffer, and file. The initial design of the device and process objects will most likely need adjustment to support their relationship with the refined view of the kernel. Various trade-offs will have to be evaluated and early ideas will have to be changed as the complete system design evolves.

It takes some practice for a programmer who is used to decomposing a design into functions to get used to designing in objects. Once a programmer catches on to the object-oriented way of thinking, however, she or he should be careful not to overdo it. As in the earlier example that creates a sorted list instead of sorting a list, it is usually possible to invent an object type to satisfy any purpose. Proliferation of concocted object types obscures a program's design. A good object-oriented design clearly corresponds to the problem that the program is to solve, making the program easy to understand, implement, and maintain.

6.3 Object Types as Modules

In object-oriented programming, the elements of a problem correspond to design elements that are the object types forming the program modules. An advantage of this method of building programs is that there is a conceptual continuity across all phases of program construction. The resulting object type modules can also be easily extracted from one program and reused in another.

The conceptual structure of a program not only remains the same from problem description through implementation but also remains the same during refinement of a design. Once the object types are identified, the design is refined by adding details to these types. This contrasts with top-down stepwise refinement of a function, in which the higher level design is decomposed into a different structure. Having a complete design structure before all details are known aids rapid prototyping. Prototype implementations of object types can be achieved by putting in a few operations and hiding unfinished details, allowing the feasibility of a design to be tested early. Being able to build prototypes quickly reduces the cost of trial-and-error design.

Consider a word processing program that manipulates strings. Once the need for a string object type is identified in the program design, a `class String` can be quickly implemented by using simple data structures and existing library routines, as in our first example of `class String` in Chapter 3. This simple version of `String` can be used in prototyping to identify exactly what string operations are needed. Adding operations to the prototype `class String` parallels the refinement of details in the program design. Once the feasibility of a design is proved, a more sophisticated implementation of `String`, like the one in Chapter 4, can replace the prototype version.

Since object-oriented design is not top down, the resulting program modules are more independent and, therefore, easier to reuse. A module is not incorporated into the design hierarchy of a particular program and so does not depend on a particular program structure. The object type module is an implementation of an element in a particular problem domain instead of a subfunction of one solution to a problem. The module can, therefore, be used for any program in the same or an overlapping problem domain. For example, `String` can be reused in any program that needs a type to represent words or text.

Another aspect of module reuse is the easy extensibility and specialization of object types by inheritance. The original module remains untouched as new functionality is added in a derived type. Modules that are general object types can be reused for many variations of a problem, and code that uses only the general properties of the base class still works with specialized versions.

6.4 Dynamic Object-Oriented Style

Object-oriented programming is associated with a programming style consisting of runtime creation of objects and dynamic binding of operations on objects. This style of programming is associated with interactive object-oriented languages and systems like Flavors and Smalltalk. These systems were designed for runtime flexibility and have proved to be successful tools for prototyping and immediate problem solving.

It is possible to write object-oriented programs in C++ that consist entirely of runtime creation of object instances and that have dynamic binding of operations on objects with virtual functions. The creation of objects and invocation of object operations is done from within the text of a compiled program. Although the virtual function calls are dynamically bound, they are statically type checked. What C++ does not have in interactive flexibility, it makes up for in strong compile-time type checking and efficient execution.

Dynamic object-oriented programming is often used for simulations. Object types are implemented to simulate different entities in the problem. Object instances are then set in motion to enact the simulation. The objects interact by invoking operations on one another and by creating new objects that enter the simulation. The rest of this chapter presents a program simulating airplane traffic at an airport.

The C++ "task" library is used in the airport simulation to allow different actions to run as coroutines. The library keeps track of simulated time and provides the control mechanisms for scheduling and running the routines. The coroutines in the simulation are the constructors of class `task` objects, or classes derived from `task`. When a `task` object is created, the execution of the constructor is scheduled under library control. The task library implements nonpreemptive scheduling, so each task must give up control on its own to give other tasks a chance to run. In this simulation, task execution is controlled by the `task` member function

```
void task::delay( int )
```

which suspends the execution of a task for a given number of simulated time units, allowing the library to schedule another coroutine for continued execution. A library global variable, `clock`, keeps track of the passage of time. The function

```
void task::cancel( int )
```

terminates the execution of a task.

The library also provides classes for implementing queues. The class types `qhead` and `qtail` are separate in the task library because they need to be able to function independently for the different tasks that put objects on and take objects off queues. The queue functions we use are

```
qtail *qhead::tail()
```

for getting the `qtail` coupled with a particular `qhead`,

```
int qtail::put( object * )
```

which adds an object to the end of the queue, and,

```
object *qhead::get()
```

which removes an object from the head of a queue. Functions to check if a queue is full or empty are

```
int qtail::rdspace()
```

which returns the amount of spaces left for adding more objects to the queue, and

```
int qhead::rdcount()
```

which gives the number of objects already on the queue. The class type `object` is the base type from which all queue elements must be derived. Since `task` and other classes in the task library have `object` as their root base type, objects of these types can be placed on queues.

The task library also provides random number generators. We use `class urand` to provide random numbers uniformly distributed over a given range, through the function

```
int urand::draw()
```

The `main` function creates an `Airport` task object, lets it run for a period of simulated time, then closes down the simulation and returns. As soon as the `Airport` is created `main` itself becomes a task running as a co-routine with the other tasks. The task system pointer `thistask` always refers to the currently running task and is needed to control the execution of `main` as a coroutine.

```
#include "Airport.h"

main() {
    Airport *ap = new Airport;
    thistask->delay( 5000 );
    delete ap;
    thistask->resultis(0);
}
```

The airport header file itself includes the header of the task library. The object types for the simulation are built from the task library types.

```
/* This is Airport.h */
#include "task.h"

class Plane : object {
    static int fltcount;
    long start;
    int fltno;
  public:
    Plane() { fltno = ++fltcount; }
    long howlong() { return clock - start; }
    void set() { start = clock; }
    int flt() { return fltno; }
};
```

```
class PlaneQ {
    qhead *head;
    qtail *tail;
  public:
    PlaneQ() {  head = new qhead( ZMODE, 50 );
              tail = head->tail();}
    void put( Plane *p ) { p->set();
              tail->put( (object*)p );}
    Plane *get() { return (Plane *)head->get(); }
    int isroom() { return tail->rdspace(); }
    int notempty() { return head->rdcount(); }
};

class AirControl : public task  {
    PlaneQ  *landing, *inair;
  public:
    AirControl( PlaneQ *, PlaneQ * );
};

class GroundControl : public task {
    PlaneQ *takingoff, *onground;
  public:
    GroundControl( PlaneQ*, PlaneQ* );
};

class Airport : public task {
    PlaneQ  *takingoff, *landing, *inair, *onground;
    AirControl *acontrol;
    GroundControl *gcontrol;
  public:
    Airport();
    ~Airport();
};
```

The different object types are `Plane`, for airplanes; `PlaneQ`, for queues of airplanes waiting to use the airport facilities; `AirControl`, for directing airplanes in the air around the airport; `GroundControl`, for directing airplanes on the ground; and `Airport`, which consists of airplane queues and controllers for directing air and ground traffic. The `Airport` itself handles the control of the runway.

A `Plane` is derived from `object`, the base type that is manipulated by the task system. The implementation of `Plane` keeps track of flight time and delay information using the task library variable `clock`, which measures simulated time.

`PlaneQ` encapsulates a `qhead` and `qtail`, which implement a queue for holding planes. A `PlaneQ` is set up so that it holds fifty planes and so that a `get` on an empty queue returns a null pointer. (Queues can also be created so that a `get` on an empty queue suspends the calling task.)

`AirControl`, `GroundControl`, and `Airport` are all `tasks`. When instances of these types are created, their constructors run as coroutines.

The `Airport` constructor creates the plane queues on which planes await service, and then creates the control tasks that feed the queues. It then goes into an infinite loop that runs until the `Airport` task is canceled. The airport serves one plane for landing and one plane for take off every ten simulated time units. If there are not already planes waiting, the planes are taken off the queues. Reports on the progress of a plane are made using `printf`. The reality of planes running out of fuel while waiting for landing is inelegantly simulated by a crash landing, removing the plane from the simulation.

```
Airport::Airport() {

    takingoff = new PlaneQ;
    inair = new PlaneQ;
    landing = new PlaneQ;
    onground = new PlaneQ;

    acontrol = new AirControl( landing, inair );
    gcontrol = new GroundControl( takingoff, onground);

    Plane *tp=0, *lp=0; // waiting planes
    int maxwait = 30;

    for(;;){
        delay( 10 );
        if( !lp ) lp = landing->get();
```

```
        if( !tp ) tp = takingoff->get();
        if( lp ){
           if( onground->isroom() ) {
              printf( "flight %d landing \n",
                 lp->flt());
              onground->put( lp );
              lp = 0;
           }
           else if( lp->howlong() > maxwait ) {
              printf( "flight %d crash landing!\n",
                 lp->flt());
              delete lp;
              lp = 0;
           } else
              printf( "flight %d landing delayed \n",
                 lp->flt());
        }
        if( tp ) {
           if( inair->isroom() ) {
              printf( "flight %d taking off\n",
                    tp->flt());
              inair->put( tp );
              tp = 0;
           } else
              printf( "flight %d take off delayed \n",
                    lp ->flt());
        }
     }
  }
```

The `Airport` destructor cancels the `AirControl` task so that no more planes are scheduled for landing. It delays until all waiting planes have landed, and then cancels the remaining tasks running the airport.

```
Airport::~Airport() {
    acontrol->cancel(0);
    while( landing->notempty() )
        thistask->delay( 10 );
    gcontrol->cancel(0);
    printf("Airport Closed\n");
    cancel(0);
}
```

The `AirControl` schedules arriving planes for landing every one to thirty time units. The varying arrival time interval is implemented using `urand`, a random number generator type provided in the task library. In this case, in which only a single airport is simulated, planes are created to be put on the landing queue or recycled from planes that have taken off from the airport.

```
AirControl:: AirControl( PlaneQ *landing,
            PlaneQ *inair ) {

    urand n( 1, 30 );

    for(;;){
        delay( n.draw() );

        Plane *p = inair->get();
        if( !p ) {
            p = new Plane;
        }
        if( landing->isroom() ) {
            printf ("flight %d arriving for landing\n",
                p->flt() );
            landing->put( p );
        } else {
            printf ("flight %d redirected\n",
                p->flt() );
            delete p;
        }
    }
}
```

The `GroundControl` takes ten to thirty time units to service a plane on the ground, and then schedules it for take off.

```
GroundControl::GroundControl( PlaneQ *takingoff,
                 PlaneQ *onground ) {

    urand n( 10, 30 );
    Plane *p = 0;

    for(;;){
        delay( n.draw() );
        if( !p ) p = onground->get();
        if( p ) {
            if( takingoff->isroom() ) {
                printf ("flight %d leaving gate\n",
                        p->flt() );
                takingoff->put( p );
                p = 0;
            } else
                printf ("flight %d delayed at gate\n",
                        p->flt() );
        }
    }
}
```

Here is the end of the output of the airport simulation:

```
flight 5 arriving for landing
flight 82 crash landing!
flight 84 arriving for landing
flight 9 landing delayed
flight 48 leaving gate
flight 9 landing
flight 48 taking off
flight 48 arriving for landing
flight 17 leaving gate
flight 83 landing
flight 17 taking off
flight 17 arriving for landing
flight 5 crash landing!
flight 84 crash landing!
flight 32 leaving gate
flight 48 landing
```

```
flight 32 taking off
flight 17 crash landing!
flight 60 leaving gate
Airport Closed
```

Frequent crash landings occurred in the simulation. This seems not to be caused by a backlog of landing planes, but by the short delay tolerance and a ground queue backlog. Different values can be tried for the maximum landing delay, ground service waits, arrival interval, and queue sizes to see the effects on the occurrence of crashes, delays, and redirected flights.

6.5 Exercises

Exercise 6-1. Add better handling of emergency landings to the airport simulation. □

Exercise 6-2. Implement the `Intlist` abstract data type used in the example in the first section of this chapter. Implement the `Sortedintlist` type as a type derived from `Intlist`. □

Exercise 6-3. Redesign the air and ground control modules in the airport simulation to be specialized versions of a control type. □

Exercise 6-4. †Extend the airport simulation to include a national flight control that routes flights among different airports. □

Exercise 6-5. Many applications are conceptualized as moving from an initial state through a sequence of states in response to input. At each state, some action is performed. For example, automated banking programs, airline reservation systems, and compiler lexical analyzers can be conceptualized in this way. Typically, the state transitions are encoded in a table indexed by the current state and an integer code corresponding to the input. For each new state, the action corresponding to that state is performed.

What are the advantages and potential problems of this approach?

An alternative framing of this conceptualization is to create a state object that encapsulates all the semantics for a given state, including next state and action to be performed.

What are the advantages of the object-oriented approach in this situation? What are the disadvantages?

Design an automated banking application, and implement it using both approaches. □

CHAPTER 7: **Storage Management**

In many programming texts, the topic of storage management is often considered unimportant or an area that is handled by the language or programming environment. Proper control of storage management is essential to the correctness of an application, however, and can be important to its efficiency.

Inefficient allocation and freeing of memory can contribute greatly to the inefficiency of an application by causing too many system calls to get more memory, by fragmenting available storage and causing "thrashing" as pages are continually swapped in and out of memory, or by running out of memory entirely. Ad hoc attempts to address these inefficiencies can lead to incorrect storage management, such as premature freeing or accidental aliasing of a block of memory.

Storage management needs are application-specific. In some cases, all storage management needs are statically determined; in others they are almost entirely dynamic. Frequently, there is application-specific information of which one can take advantage to produce an efficient storage management scheme. Although C++ provides default general storage management, it also provides the ability to customize storage management for a given problem area, class type, or application.

7.1 General-Purpose Storage Management

Operators `new` and `delete` are predeclared, standard library functions that manage free store or "heap" memory.

```
extern void *operator new( size_t );
extern void operator delete( void * );
```

`operator new` returns a block of free store of at least the number of bytes specified in its argument, and `operator delete` frees a block of free

179

store previously allocated by `operator new`.

```
void
allocer() {
    Thing *tp = new Thing;
    dostuffwith( tp );
    delete tp;
}
```

The size of the object to be allocated is determined by examination of the operand of the `new` operator and passed as an implicit argument to `operator new`. As with other overloaded operators, we can also invoke `new` and `delete` explicitly,

```
int *
hunkoints()
    { return (int *)operator new(sizeof(int)*16384); }
```

but the prefix notation is generally clearer and safer.

```
int *
hunkoints()
    { return new int[16384]; }
```

To give more control over memory allocation, a standard function, `set_new_handler`, can be used to specify a function to be called if `operator new` should fail. The argument to `set_new_handler` is a pointer to a function that takes no arguments and returns no result, and `set_new_handler` returns the previous argument. Until either it is able to allocate the requested memory or `set_new_handler` is supplied with a null argument, `operator new` will iteratively call the function set by `set_new_handler`.

```
void
give_up() {
    error( "ran out of memory!" );
    exit( 1 );
}
```

```
void
scavenge() {
    garbage_collect();
    set_new_handler( give_up );
}

void
allocer() {
    void (*saved_handler)() = set_new_handler(scavenge);
    Thing *tp = new Thing;
    dostuffwith( tp );
    set_new_handler( saved_handler );
    delete tp;
}
```

Now if `operator new` fails to allocate the requested amount of memory, it will first call `scavenge` to free up memory. If `scavenge` fails to free up enough memory to satisfy the request, then `give_up` prints a message and terminates the program.

The behavior of the default `new_handler` function on a particular platform may be to throw an exception (see Chapter 8), but setting `new_handler` to null will cause `operator new` to return null on failure. In recent practice, however, program code does not typically check that the return result from `operator new` is non-null, and memory allocation errors are handled by other means (see Chapter 8).

This use of `new_handler` is a very flexible mechanism, and the standard library operators `new` and `delete` serve for most applications.

In exceptional circumstances, however, we can override the standard versions by supplying our own versions of `operator new` and `operator delete`. These user-defined versions are used in place of the standard versions.

For example, `operator new` does not guarantee that the storage it returns is initialized to all zeros although, in short runs of a program under some operating systems, storage may just happen to be zeroed. If code takes advantage of this ostensible zeroing, then errors may not be caught during testing, and will appear in longer production runs of the program. We might, therefore, want to supply development versions of `new` and `delete` to fill returned storage with ''garbage'' in order to catch errors of this sort early in testing.

```
extern void *malloc( unsigned );
extern void free( void * );

extern void *
operator new( size_t sz ) {
    char *p = (char *) malloc( sz );
    if( p ) {
        for( int i = 0; i < sz; i++ )
            p[i] = '~';
    }
    return p;
}

extern void
operator delete( void *p )
    { if( p ) free( p ); }
```

Note that `set_new_handler` will no longer have any effect on the behavior of `operator new` unless we explicitly code it; `set_new_handler` is simply part of the implementation of the standard library `operator new`.

In general, it is best not to replace the standard versions of `operator new` and `operator delete`. The standard versions of these operators are highly optimized for general-purpose memory management, and user-defined versions are unlikely to be able to provide better general-purpose performance. Special-purpose versions of **new** and **delete** may achieve better performance for a particular application, but they are just as likely to fare worse, or even to introduce bugs into programs incorporating general-purpose library code that assumes the semantics of the standard operators **new** and **delete**.

Like most other operators, `operator new` can be overloaded. For example, we could supply a version of `operator new`, similar to the previous version, that allows one to specify with precisely what "garbage" the allocated memory is to be filled.

```
extern void *
operator new( size_t n, const String &fill );
```

All versions of `operator new` must return `void *` and have a first argument of type `size_t` that specifies the minimum number of bytes of storage to be allocated. Any number and type of additional arguments may then be specified. Standard overload resolution is used to determine which version of operator new is to be called.

```
SortedCollection *cp = new SortedCollection;
delete cp;
String fill = "<pure and unadulterated garbage>";
cp = new ( fill ) SortedCollection;
delete cp;
```

In the first allocation above, the single-argument version of `operator new` is called to allocate the storage for a `SortedCollection` object, after which the default `SortedCollection` constructor is invoked to perform initialization of the object. The second allocation matches the two-argument version of `operator new`. Notice that the second and subsequent (if any) actual arguments to `operator new` are passed in an argument list that follows the `new` keyword. If there are, in addition, object initializers, they are appended after the type name in the usual manner.

```
String *sp = new ( fill ) String( "Hello, World!" );
```

The first argument list specifies arguments to `operator new`, the second argument list specifies arguments to the `String` constructor.

Unlike `operator new`, `operator delete` can not be overloaded. We must, therefore, be careful to ensure that the single implementation of `operator delete` works with all versions of `operator new` or, more to the point, that all versions of `operator new` work correctly with the standard version of `operator delete`.

```
void *
operator new( size_t n, const String &pat ) {
    char *p = (char *) ::operator new( n );
    // See Exercise 7-7.
    const char *pattern = pat;
    if( !pattern || !pattern[0] )
        pattern = "\0";
    const char *f = pattern;
```

```
    for( int i = 0; i < n; i++ ) {
        if( !*f )
            f = pattern;
        p[i] = *f++;
    }
    return p;
}
```

The implementation of our overloaded version of `operator new` uses the standard versions of `new` and `delete` to perform memory management and simply adds additional behavior.

A commonly used overloaded version of `operator new` that is provided as standard on some systems is the "placement" version.

```
void *
operator new( size_t, void *placement )
    { return placement; }
```

This version of `operator new` simply returns its second argument and is used to place an object at a specific location.

```
void * const ports_loc = (void *) 0x00400000;

Ports *ports = new ( ports_loc ) Ports;
```

This declaration has the effect of initializing the storage at location `ports_loc` as an object of type `Ports`. It is also necessary to activate the `Ports` destructor on the object referred to by `ports` at the end of its lifetime. Ordinarily, objects allocated with a `new` are deallocated with a `delete`, and the destructor is implicitly activated prior to the deletion. However, the standard `operator delete` assumes that the storage to be deleted was allocated by the standard `operator new`; invoking `delete` on the object referred to by `ports` is likely to lead to disaster. In cases like this, a destructor may be called explicitly.

```
    ports->~Ports();
```

Another use of the placement version of `operator new` and explicit destructor call is to reinitialize an already allocated object, rather than to initialize unstructured storage for the first time.

```
File *f = new File( "scratchfile" );
// ... use f to create aliases throughout code
// ... file changed in application
// release current file resource
f->~File();
// create new object at old address
f = new ( f ) File( "new_scratch" );
// ... continue execution
delete f; // final deletion pairs with initial new
```

The placement version of `operator new` and the ability to invoke destructors explicitly provide useful functionality but are potential sources of errors and should, therefore, be used carefully. Ordinarily, we strive to pair every use of `operator new` with a corresponding use of `operator delete` and to activate destructors implicitly rather than explicitly. Performing a deletion of memory ''allocated'' via a placement or implicitly activating a destructor for an object that has already been destroyed explicitly would probably cause errors.

7.2 Class-Specific Storage Management

The implementations of `new` and `delete` we have seen so far have been general-purpose. Like the standard library versions, they are meant to serve for all types in all cases. However, type or application-specific knowledge can be employed to speed up or simplify memory management significantly. To take advantage of specialized knowledge without affecting the standard memory management operators, C++ provides the ability to define class-specific versions of `operator new` and `operator delete`. When declared within a class definition, operators `new` and `delete` are static member functions; that is, they have no implicit `this` pointer and require no object of the class in order to be invoked. This follows from their intended use to allocate and free objects of a given class type.

For example, class `complex` has a very small and simple implementation. We can speed up memory management significantly with member `new` and `delete` operators that take advantage of the implementation-specific details.

```
class complex {
    double re, im;
  public:
    void *operator new( size_t );
    void operator delete( void * );
    // ...
};
```

These operators are invoked whenever an object of type `complex` is allocated or deleted, whether or not the allocation or deletion is performed in the scope of class `complex`.

```
#include <complex.h>

main() {
    complex *cp = new complex( 12 );
    int *ip = new int;
    *ip = 12;
    complex cgross = *cp * *ip;
}
```

The cp pointer refers to storage allocated by `complex::operator new`, whereas `ip` refers to storage allocated by `::operator new`. In addition, `cgross` is an automatic and did not require a call to any `operator new` prior to its initialization.

We implement storage management for `complex` by allocating elements of a static array. Freed elements are maintained on a freelist. The implementation of `complex::operator new` first checks the freelist for a previously allocated and freed element. If there are none, but there are elements of the array that have not yet been allocated, one is allocated. Otherwise, `operator new` fails and returns null.

```
static const int MAX = 100;

static class Rep {
    static Rep *free;
    static int num_used;
```

```
    union {
    double store[2];
    Rep *next;
    };
    friend class complex;
} mem[MAX];

void *
complex::operator new( size_t ) {
    if( Rep::free ) {
        Rep *tmp = Rep::free;
        Rep::free = Rep::free->next;
        return tmp->store;
    }
    else if( Rep::num_used < MAX )
        return mem[ Rep::num_used++ ].store;
    else
        return 0;
}
```

The implementation of `complex::operator delete` just adds the element of the array being freed to the head of the freelist.

```
void
complex::operator delete( void *p ) {
    ((Rep *)p)->next = Rep::free;
    Rep::free = (Rep *)p;
}
```

Note that `complex::operator new` does not check the value of its argument but always returns storage large enough to hold an object of type `complex`. The implicit assumption is that no class will be derived from class `complex`. This may be a good assumption, but, if it were not the case, we could be in trouble.

```
class Point3 : public complex {
    // a point in 3-space
    double z;
  public:
    // ...
};
Point3 *p = new Point3;
```

Since `Point3` inherits `new` and `delete` along with the other members of class `complex`, the constructor call for `Point3` invokes `complex::operator new` and returns storage large enough for a `complex` but not necessarily large enough for a `Point3`.

We can go further in designing class-specific `new` and `delete` than considering just the properties of the type; we can also design a memory allocation scheme that depends on properties of the application as a whole.

Consider the calculator program for which we designed the `Node` hierarchy of Chapter 5. Suppose our calculator program builds only a single abstract syntax tree at a time, evaluates it, and deletes the entire tree. Given this, we can redesign memory management to be much more efficient.

```
class Node {
  protected:
    Node() {}
  public:
    // ...
    void *operator new( size_t );
    void operator delete( void * ) {}
    static void flush();    // recover all mem
    enum { SZ = 1000 };
    class Buf {
        Buf *next;
        char mem[SZ];
        friend class Node;
    };
  private:
    static Buf b;    // initial buffer
    static Buf *bp; // ->current buffer
    static char *memp; // ->current pos in buf
    // ...
};
```

`Node::operator new` and `Node::operator delete` are inherited by classes derived from `Node`, so we must either provide different versions of these operators for each derived class or make them sufficiently general to serve all node types. Here, we do the latter.

```
void *
Node::operator new( size_t sz ) {
    if( memp+sz > &bp->mem[SZ] )
        if( bp->next ) {
            bp = bp->next;
            memp = bp->mem;
        }
        else if( bp = bp->next = new Buf )
            memp = bp->mem;
        else
            return 0;
    char *r = memp;
    memp += sz;
    return r;
}
```

We start with a statically allocated buffer whose size we estimate will be sufficient for most runs of the application and allocate additional buffers from free store as needed. Note that the use of `new` to allocate the overflow buffers refers to the global `operator new` because the buffer is not of type `Node` or a type derived from `Node`.

The implementation of `operator delete` takes advantage of the fact that any use of `delete` is to release the entire abstract syntax tree. Therefore, `operator delete` does nothing, and we provide a static member function to release all memory.

```
Node::Buf Node::b;
Node::Buf *Node::bp = &b;
char *Node::memp = b.mem;

void
Node::flush()
    { bp = &b; memp = b.mem; }

// ...
int
limited_use() {
    // Evaluate -11+21*93
    Node *np =
        new Plus(
            // ...
        );
```

```
        int result = np->eval();
        delete np;    // activate destructors
        Node::flush();   // reclaim memory
        return result;
    }
```

We hold on to any additional buffers we may have allocated in order to prevent their reallocation in subsequent uses of the `Node` hierarchy.

This version of `new` and `delete` is much faster than the standard one, but it is also tightly coupled to the way we use abstract syntax trees in a specific application.

The `new` operator may also be overloaded within a class. For example, we may require the ability to allocate `Node` objects within various different memory arenas with different properties.

```
    class Arena;

    class Node {
      public:
        // See Exercise 7-4.
        void *operator new( size_t );
        void *operator new( size_t, Arena * );
        void operator delete( void * );
        // ...
    };
    // ...
    extern Arena *ephemeral;
    extern Arena *persistent;
    extern Arena *shared;
    // ...
    Node *np1 = new ( shared ) Int( 12 );
    Node *np2 = new ( persistent ) Int( 2 );
    Node *np3 = new Int( 3 ); // default arena
```

The single implementation of `operator delete` must be capable of deleting storage allocated by any of the overloaded instances of `operator new`.

Class-specific `new` and `delete` specify the semantics of allocating and freeing objects of a specific class type and, unless explicitly overridden, of classes derived from that class type. For some types, the proper allocation semantics are to disallow heap allocation entirely.

Consider the design of a resource controller type. The idea is to allocate a resource "handle" on the runtime stack that controls the seizing and releasing of some resource (file handle, database lock, shared memory segment, etc.) The implementation takes advantage of the semantics of constructor and destructor activation to control the resource. Initialization of the resource handle has the side effect of seizing the resource, while destruction of the resource handle has the side effect of releasing the resource. If the resource handle is allocated as an automatic on the runtime stack, or as a static, the seizing and releasing of the resource are automatic as well.

```
class ResourceHandle {
  protected:
    ResourceHandle();
  public:
    virtual ~ResourceHandle() = 0;
  protected:
    void *operator new( size_t ) { return 0; }
    void operator delete( void * ) {}
  private:
    // ...
};
```

Here we have created an abstract base class that encapsulates the essential properties of a resource handle. Classes derived from `ResourceHandle` supply a constructor to allocate a resource and a destructor to release a resource, and inherit the protected memory allocation operators. Since they are protected, only members and friends of classes derived from `ResourceHandle` are able to access them; other attempts to allocate objects derived from `ResourceHandle` on the heap are flagged as errors at compile time.

```
class FileHandle : public ResourceHandle {
    FILE *fp;
  public:
    FileHandle( const char *filename,
        const char *filemode = "r" )
        : fp( fopen( filename, filemode ) ) {}
    ~FileHandle() { if( fp ) fclose( fp ); }
    operator FILE *() { return fp; }
};
```

```
FileHandle globfile( "cfront.h", "r+" );   // OK, static

ptrdiff_t
filediff( const Pathname &path ) {
   FileHandle fh( path ); // OK, auto
   FileHandle *fhp =
      new FileHandle( path );   // error, heap!
   return fh - *fhp;
}
```

We noted earlier that class-specific new and delete are invoked only to perform storage management of objects of their class type, and not for objects of other types, even if the allocation occurs within the scope of the class defining the operators. This reasoning also applies to arrays of class objects; because an array of class objects is not a class object, the class-specific storage management operators are not implicitly invoked for arrays.

```
complex *vector = new complex[3];
```

The allocation above invokes `::operator new` rather than `complex::operator new`.

In general, it is preferable not to allocate arrays of any but the simplest classes and the predefined types. Much of the utility of classes lies in inheritance and dynamic binding, the use of which would be severely restricted in an array of like objects. Generally, an array of pointers to class objects is used in preference to an array of class objects themselves.

```
Node *cses = new Node *[MAX];
```

Additionally, there may be restrictions on the set of initializers that may be supplied to the objects in an allocated array. Consult your C++ compiler's documentation for details on array allocation and deallocation.

7.3 Copy Semantics

A constructor that can be invoked with an argument of its own class's type specifies how to initialize an object of that class with another object of that class. An assignment operator that can be invoked with an argument of its own class's type specifies how to assign an object of that class to another object of that class. Together, these operations specify the ''copy semantics'' of the class. For a class `X`, these operations are typically declared in the following manner.

```
class X {
    // ...
    X( const X & );
    X &operator =( const X & );
    // ...
};
```

We have already seen uses of user-defined copy semantics. The `String` type of Chapter 4 uses a `String(const String&)` constructor and a member `operator =(const String&)` to ensure that whenever a `String` is copied (in an initialization and in an assignment, respectively) the correct reference counts are maintained in the underlying `String::Rep` objects.

The default implementation of copy initialization is to initialize one object with another, member by member; the default implementation of copy assignment is to assign one object to another, member by member. For `String` objects, the default implementation is incorrect because it does not maintain the correct reference counts. However, the default implementation is perfectly appropriate for `complex` objects, and `class complex` provides no explicit copy semantics. The `SortedCollection` type of Chapter 4 presents a third possibility. The default member-by-member copy semantics would produce incorrect results under later implementations of the type, but copying the potentially large collection is considered too costly and of little use. Our approach there was to declare the copy operations as private members of the class. The effect is to prevent copying of `SortedCollection` objects, since any attempt to do so would cause a compile time error in the invocation of a private member function. Defining copy semantics for a class states that the operation of copying objects of that class type must be carefully controlled and that the default copy semantics are not appropriate.

Note that the default copy semantics do not necessarily imply "bitwise" copy, that is, simply copying one region of memory onto another. Rather, the default member-by-member copy respects any copy semantics defined by base classes or members.

```
class Text {
   Text *next;
   String phrase;
 public:
   // ...
};

Text a( "Hello, World!" );
Text b( a );
a = b;
```

In the initialization of b by a, and in the assignment of b to a, the String member's copy constructor and assignment operator are invoked, respectively, as part of the copy operation. The compiler-provided operations perform as if defined as follows.

```
inline
Text::Text( const Text &t )
    : next( t.next ),   // bitwise
      phrase( t.phrase ) // String(const String &)
      {}

inline
Text &Text::operator =( const Text &t ) {
   next = t.next;       // bitwise
   phrase = t.phrase;  // operator =(const String &)
}
```

The compiler will also define copy operations if objects of that class contain internal compiler-provided mechanism that could be rendered invalid by a bitwise copy. Specifically, classes that have virtual functions or virtual base classes will also cause the compiler to generate a copy constructor and a copy assignment operator if none is defined explicitly.

In a similar vein, the compiler will also define a default constructor and a destructor under certain circumstances. If a class has no explicit constructor declaration, but has base classes or members that have default constructors, or has virtual functions or virtual base classes, then the compiler will implicitly define a default constructor that invokes the default constructors for the base class subobjects and members and performs the correct initializations of the internal object mechanisms that support virtual functions and virtual base classes. If a class has no explicit destructor declaration, but contains base classes or members that have destructors, then the compiler will implicitly define a destructor that invokes the destructors for the members and base class subobjects.

In some cases, as with class `complex`, it is permissible and correct to rely on bitwise copy semantics or to allow the compiler to provide copy operations implicitly. Each such case should be examined carefully to determine whether the default semantics are correct for the class's implementation, and any change in implementation should provoke a re-examination. There is, however, little advantage in allowing the compiler to provide the implementations of the default constructor and destructor for a class, and these should generally be provided explicitly.

7.4 Temporaries and Efficiency

The `String` class of Chapter 4 provides a single-argument constructor which may be used to provide conversions from a `char *` to a `String`. The conversion is invoked implicitly as needed.

```
class String {
    // ...
    String( const char * );
    friend int
        operator ==( const String &, const String & );
    // ...
};
// ...
String logfile;
//...
if( logfile == "/etc/accesses" )
    // ...
```

In order to match the `==` operator, the compiler has to allocate a temporary of type `String` and initialize it with the right argument using `String`'s single-argument constructor. The temporary is then used to initialize the second `const String &` formal argument. At the end of the expression, the `String` destructor is activated for the temporary.

This behavior is correct, but a plethora of such conversions, and their concomitant initialization and destruction, can cause efficiency problems. If the efficiency of a particular function invocation is a consideration, then one can add additional overloaded instances of the function in order to circumvent the creation of temporaries for conversions.

```
class String {
   // ...
   friend int
      operator ==( const String &, const String & );
   friend int
      operator ==( const String &, const char * );
   friend int
      operator ==( const char *, const String & );
   // ...
};
```

Now any combination of `String` and `char *` arguments will result in an exact match and avoid the creation of a temporary. In general, however, the advantage of a simple and clear interface takes precedence over minor questions of efficiency.

The C++ compiler itself may attempt optimization at the level of class temporaries in the name of efficiency. Consider the following declaration.

```
String notatemp = String( "Am I a temp?" );
```

Although the outward meaning of the declaration may seem to indicate that a temporary `String` object first be created and initialized before being used to initialize `notatemp` as the argument to the `String( const String & )` constructor, it is legitimate and common for a C++ compiler to avoid the temporary generation and simply initialize `notatemp` with the character string.

More involved transformations may occur in the case of formal argument initialization and function return. Consider initializing a formal argument with an actual argument. In some cases, a constructor or conversion operator is invoked to convert the actual argument into a value of the correct type for the formal argument. This may involve the caller's creating a temporary object in which to create the value before copying it onto the formal argument.

```
void f( complex );
f( 12 );
```

In converting the integer `12` into a `complex` value, a temporary `complex` object may be created in the caller and initialized with the class `complex` constructor. The value of the temporary would then be copied onto the formal argument. However, the compiler may also elect to avoid creation of the temporary and simply use the integer actual argument to construct a `complex` in the called function.

The compiler may apply even more complex transformations, and the programmer is warned not to depend on any side effects produced as the result of initialization or destruction of temporary objects, as these may be transformed or removed by the compiler.

7.5 Operator ->

Storage management is concerned not only with allocation and freeing of storage but also with accessing it. Applications frequently require code sequences that do some processing either before or after a storage access.

```
do something
access storage
do something else
```

Since these code sequences are not enforced in an automatic way, they can be left out either inadvertently or as an ''optimization.''

```
class Info {
    void f();
    // ...
};

Info *p;  // ALWAYS check that p is non-null!!!
// ...
void
process_Info() {
    // p is usually non-null...
    p->f();
    // ...
}
```

The clever optimization in `process_Info` leads to disaster.

To help deal with problems of this sort, C++ allows the -> operator to be overloaded, giving the ability to create ''smart'' pointers that can encapsulate both checking and access semantics. Like operators (), [], and =, `operator` -> must be a member function. It must be declared to take no argument and to return either a class type that has `operator` -> defined or a pointer to a class type.

Notice that, although the predefined -> operator is binary, user-defined `operator` -> is declared as unary. The idea is that a user-defined `operator` -> produces, either directly or indirectly, a pointer to an object of class type. This pointer is then used with the predefined -> operator to access a member of that class.

```
class InfoPtr {
    static Info null_info;
    Info *p;
  public:
    InfoPtr( Info *ip = 0 ) : p( ip ) {}
    Info *operator ->() { return p ? p : &null_info; }
};
```

This is one solution to our previous problem; `InfoPtr` is a smart pointer type that never returns a null pointer value to be used in a reference. In addition, it disallows any pointer operations, like ++, +, and so on, that could lead to a bad address.

```
InfoPtr p;
// ...
void
process_Info() {
    p->f();   // safe
    // ...
}
```

The access `p->f` first invokes `InfoPtr::operator ->` on p, producing a value of type `Info *`, which is then used to access the member `Info::f`.

`operator ->` can also be declared to return a class type that defines an `operator ->`.

```
class InfoLog {
    InfoPtr &p;
  public:
    InfoLog( InfoPtr &ip ) : p( ip ) {}
    InfoPtr &operator ->() {
        fprintf( logfile, "accessing an InfoPtr" );
        return p;
    }
};
```

An `InfoLog` object behaves like an `InfoPtr` object on use, except that it logs a message before performing a safe access.

```
extern InfoPtr p;
InfoLog wp = p;
// ...
wp->f();
```

The access **wp->f** first invokes **InfoLog::operator ->**, which prints
a message and returns an **InfoPtr**. Then **InfoPtr::operator ->** is
invoked, returning an **Info *** , which is used to access **Info::f**.

As a more realistic example of the use of smart pointers, suppose we have
a file of records on disk, and we want to be able to write applications that use
these records as if they were elements of an in-memory array, without being
concerned with system-dependent functions of reading and writing disk
records. Since there is a large number of records, however, we cannot simply
read them all into memory, and, in any case, relatively few records are examined by any given application, and fewer still are changed. We cannot afford
the overhead of reading and writing a large number of disk records.

We approach this problem by providing two types. The first represents a
file of records, and the second is a smart pointer to a file record.

```
struct rec { // a disk record
    int key;
    int value;
    // ...
};

class File {
    FILE *fp;
    Sary *hd;
    rec *operator [](int);
  public:
    File( const char * );
    ~File();
    friend class Ptr;
};
```

A user creates a file object by supplying the path name of the file to be
opened. The **FILE** type and the routines for opening, closing, reading, and
writing files are system dependent. Here, we use the **stdio** functions.

```
File::File( const char *fname )
    : fp( fopen( fname, "r+" ) ), hd( 0 ) {}
```

Since we expect to read and write relatively few records, we implement `File` as a sparse array. Our sparse array is an unordered linked list of index, record pairs.

```
class Sary {
    Sary *next;
    int index;
    rec *p;
    Sary( int, Sary *, FILE * );
    friend class File;
};
```

Thus, a `File` consists of a system-dependent file descriptor and a sparse array of file records. `File::operator []` creates elements of the sparse array whenever there is an attempt to index an element not present in the array.

```
rec *
File::operator []( int i ) {
    for( Sary *sp = hd; sp; sp = sp->next )
        if( sp->index == i )
            break;
    if( !sp )
        sp = hd = new Sary( i, hd, fp );
    return sp->p;
}
```

The sparse array node constructor creates the node and reads in the relevant record from disk. In addition, it makes a copy of the record for later comparison. The disk record is not updated if it has not been changed.

```
Sary::Sary( int i, Sary *n, FILE *fp )
    : next( n ), incex( i ) {
    const int sz = sizeof( rec );
    p = (rec *) new char[2*sz];
    fseek( fp, i*sz, 0 );
    fread( (char *)p, sz, 1, fp );
    *(p+1) = *p;
}
```

The destructor for `File` updates to disk those records that have changed, deletes the sparse array, and closes the file.

```
File::~File() {
    const int sz = sizeof(rec);
    while( hd ) {
        if( memcmp(sp->p, sp->p+1, sz) != 0 ) {
            fseek( fp, sp->index*sz, 0 );
            fwrite( (char *)sp->p, sz, 1, fp );
        }
        Sary *tmp = hd;
        hd = hd->next;
        delete tmp;
    }
    fclose( fp );
}
```

The main user interface to the `File` of database records is through a smart pointer type.

```
class Ptr {
    int index;
    File *fp;
  public:
    Ptr( File &f, int i = 0 )
        : fp(&f), index(i) {}
    rec *operator->();
    rec &operator[](int);
    rec &operator *();
    friend Ptr operator +(Ptr, int);
    friend Ptr operator +(int, Ptr);
    friend ptrdiff_t operator -(Ptr, Ptr);
    friend Ptr operator -(Ptr, int);
    Ptr &operator ++(); // prefix
    Ptr &operator --();
    Ptr &operator ++(int); // postfix
    Ptr &operator --(int);
    Ptr &operator +=(int);
    Ptr &operator -=(int);
    friend int operator ==(Ptr, Ptr);
    friend int operator !=(Ptr, Ptr);
```

```
    friend int operator <(Ptr, Ptr);
    friend int operator <=(Ptr, Ptr);
    friend int operator >(Ptr, Ptr);
    friend int operator >=(Ptr, Ptr);
};
```

A `Ptr` is implemented as a pointer to a `File` and, considering the `File` to be an array of records, a current index into the `File`. We provide all the usual operations for pointer arithmetic.

```
Ptr &
Ptr::operator ++() {
    index++;
    return *this;
}

int
operator ==( Ptr a, Ptr b )
    { return (a.index == b.index) && (a.fp == b.fp); }
```

The implementations of the other operators are similar. The arithmetic pointer operations are performed on the index of the file record, and no reference is made to the underlying `File` until necessary.

The actual work of a reference is done by `File::operator []`. Our smart pointer just returns the `File` array element corresponding to `Ptr::index`.

```
rec *
Ptr::operator ->()
    { return (*fp)[index]; }
```

For the predefined pointer types in C++, there is a correspondence between the operators `->`, `*`, and `[]`, such that `p->m` is equivalent to `(*p).m` and `*(p+i)` is equivalent to `p[i]`. As with other equivalences that exist in the predefined parts of the language, such as that between `++` and `+= 1`, if we want similar equivalences to hold for our user-defined operations, they must be defined explicitly.

```
rec &
Ptr::operator *()
    { return *(*fp)[index]; }
```

```
rec &
Ptr::operator [] ( int i )
   { return * (*fp) [index+i]; }
```

Now we can write applications. Suppose we have an ordered array of database records on disk, and we want to find and alter the value of one record.

```
void
alter( int key, const char *file, int num_recs, int val ) {
    File f = file;
    Ptr mid = f;
    Ptr low(f,0), high(f,num_recs-1);
    while( low <= high ) {
        mid = low + (high-low)/2;
        if( key < mid->key )
            high = mid - 1;
        else if( key > mid->key )
            low = mid + 1;
        else {
            mid->value = val;
            break;
        }
    }
}
```

The `alter` function opens a file and creates a sparse array of file records with the declaration of f, and creates three smart pointers into f, low, mid, and high, which are used to perform a binary search on the file records. If the record corresponding to the argument `key` is found, its value is altered. The destructor for f is activated before the return to clean up the sparse array of file records and update the disk record of the changed element.

7.6 Exercises

Exercise 7-1. Consider the effect of adding a virtual function to the `complex` type. How would this affect the efficient memory allocation scheme for complex numbers of this chapter? □

Exercise 7-2. Generalize the implementation of operators `new` and `delete` for class `complex` so that they can handle storage requests of arbitrary size. □

Exercise 7-3. Write memory management operators for a given class type that allow a particular allocation to be specified "undeleteable" so that a later invocation of `operator delete` will not delete the memory. □

Exercise 7-4. Implement `operator delete` and the overloaded `operator new(size_t)` and `operator new(size_t,Arena*)` for the `Node` class, as described in this chapter. □

Exercise 7-5. Provide an instance of `Arena` for the previous exercise that allocates an object within a shared memory segment. □

Exercise 7-6. Examine your solution to Exercise 4-28 (indexing a collection with a predicate). Are you properly reclaiming all the memory that is allocated? Is the implementation both flexible and efficient? Test your solution with the following function.

```
extern int moe( Etype );
extern int larry( Etype );
extern int curly( Etype );

void
test( SortedCollection &c ) {
   SortedCollection d;
   d = c[ moe ];
   d = c[ moe ][ larry ][ curly ];
}
```

□

Exercise 7-7. In the implementation of `operator new( size_t, const String & )` of this chapter, explain why memory was allocated with the syntax

```
char *p = ::operator new( n );
```

rather than

```
char *p = new char[n];
```

□

Exercise 7-8. †Implement the `ResourceHandle` type of this chapter. □

Exercise 7-9. Use the language features discussed in this chapter to re-implement the inorder control abstraction for binary trees of Exercise 4-21. Pay particular attention to the semantics of assignment and initialization of one inorder control abstraction with another. Provide class-specific memory allocation to improve performance. □

Exercise 7-10. †Design a generic smart pointer type that is guaranteed to point only to free store. □

Exercise 7-11. Some programming languages support offsets. An offset is a language feature analogous to a pointer; it is simply an index into a contiguous area of memory (often called an arena). A major advantage in using offsets is that the entire arena may be stored on external media and then restored to a different address without requiring change to the values of offsets.

Design an offset to a particular type. Provide the ability to allocate, write out, and read in arenas. Extend the implementation to be a family of offset types. □

Exercise 7-12. Extend the offset implementation of the previous exercise to handle multiple arenas. □

Exercise 7-13. Reimplement the `File` and `Ptr` types of this chapter to perform bounds checking. □

Exercise 7-14. †Show how `operator ->` can be used to delegate some operations of a given object to another object. Compare the use of delegation to that of inheritance. □

Exercise 7-15. †Develop a technique that will prevent users of a given class from creating automatic or static objects of that class. □

Exercise 7-16. Develop a technique for producing "future" types that calculate an interesting value in a separate thread of execution on initialization or assignment, and block access to the result until the calculation is complete. Show how one could implement architecture-independent fine-grain parallelism using this technique. Use your technique to create a "future hash table" type based on the persistent hash table type of Exercise 3-6. □

CHAPTER 8: **Libraries**

A software library is collection of program modules that is separate from any individual program. The separation of the modules into a library makes them available for use by any client program. In a traditional procedural programming environment, a software library is a collection of functions, or functions and data structures, that provide specific services. For example, there are libraries of mathematical functions, access to operating system services, data structure descriptions of standard file formats, and standard input and output routines.

There are three important benefits associated with the use of libraries in program construction. First, a library provides code from a single source. Code reuse can reduce the time required to design and code an application since, if a library already provides needed functionality, part of the work is already done. Reuse of a mature and proven library can also reduce the time required to test and debug a new program. Second, a library can provide a portable or standard interface that isolates client programs from lower-level dependencies. If environment-dependent aspects of an application are encapsulated within a library, the task of porting that application to different environments is reduced to the task of porting the library. If a standard library is used, it may already be available in many environments. Third, a library that provides an interface designed on high-level abstractions in a specific application area can reduce the difficulty of implementing programs in that area. For example, a library that provides high-level abstractions for performing database searches and updates relieves the application programmer from the details of connecting to a database, buffering, and forming query operations.

In this chapter, we discuss how the programming paradigms and C++ language features described in previous chapters extend the traditional concept of a library and support new techniques for designing and implementing libraries.

8.1 Interface Encapsulation

The design principles for abstract data types, discussed in Chapter 4, can also be applied to library interfaces. A C++ class can be used to simplify a library interface by hiding data and by grouping related functions into a conceptual unit. Encapsulating an existing library in a class provides a means to organize the interface around key abstractions in its design. Encapsulation is also a mechanism for building a higher-level abstraction from existing primitive functionality.

For example, consider the I/O functions provided in the C library `stdio`.

```
FILE *fopen( const char *, const char * );
int fclose( FILE * );
int fflush( FILE * );
int fprintf( FILE *, const char *, ... );
int fscanf( FILE *, const char *, ... );
```

One way to view these functions is as a collection of operations on file objects. Note that `fopen` fills the role of a constructor, `fclose` fills that of a destructor, and the other functions look just like member functions, even down to the (ordinarily) implicit `this` first argument.

We can define an alternative interface to make our abstraction explicit by using a class as a wrapper.

```
class File {
    FILE * const f;
  public:
    File( const char *path, const char *mode = "w" )
        : f( fopen( path, mode ) ) {}
    ~File() { fclose( f ); }
    int flush() { return fflush( f ); }
    int printf( const char *, ... );
    int scanf( const char *, ...);
    //...
};
```

The implementations of `File::printf` and `File::scanf` are complicated by the ellipsis final argument. We want the formal arguments in the definitions of the member `printf` and `scanf` functions to be used as the actual arguments to a call to the `stdio` functions `fprintf` and `fscanf` respectively. As the ellipsis parameter tells us, however, we cannot determine the number of arguments until runtime. There are several ways of dealing with this situation, most of which are environment-dependent. Here in our minimal implementation of `File::printf` we use the "varargs" facility provided by definitions in the standard header `stdarg.h`. An object of type `va_list`, `ap` in our example, holds information on how to access the arguments. Note that `va_start` initializes `ap` using the last declared argument before the ellipsis, `fmt` in our example. In addition, `va_arg` returns successive arguments from the argument list interpreted according to the type provided in the second argument of `va_arg`. Finally, `va_end` provides a normal termination of the variable-argument facility.

```
int
File::printf( const char *fmt, ... ) {
    va_list ap;
    va_start( ap, fmt );

    register int c;
    while( c = *fmt++ ) {
       if( c == '%' ) {
           switch( c = *fmt++ ) {
           case 'c': // character
               fprintf( f, "%c", va_arg( ap, int ) );
               break;
           case 'd': // decimal integer
               fprintf( f, "%d", va_arg( ap, int ) );
               break;
           case 'g': // floating
               fprintf( f, "%g", va_arg( ap, double ) );
               break;
           case 's': // character string
               fprintf( f, "%s", va_arg( ap, char* ) );
               break;
           // etc...
           }
       }
       else
           fprintf( f, "%c", c );
    }

    va_end( ap );
}
```

Now we can create and use `File` objects for `stdio`. We changed the name of the member output function from `fprintf` to `printf`, and the name of the member input function from `fscanf` to `scanf`, in order to match the names used for input and output to the predefined files `stdout` and `stdin`. Use of these routines can be thought of as I/O to default `File` objects.

```
void
tee( const char *fn ) {
    File f = fn;
    char c;
    while( scanf( "%c", &c ) != EOF ) {
        f.printf( "%c", c );
        printf( "%c", c );
    }
}
```

The `class File` encapsulation of the `stdio` library provides an explicit organization of the library interface around a file abstraction. The abstraction level of the original interface, however, is not changed. We can further encapsulate the standard file I/O functionality to build a higher-level abstraction that provides services to greatly reduce the details with which client programs need to deal. For example, the `TextInput` class below provides complete management of an input file. It handles the opening and closing of the file, iteration over the lines of text, and the management of the dynamically allocated `String` objects that hold each line for use by the client.

```
class String;
class File;

typedef void (*LineHandler)( String & );

class TextInput {
    class StringManager &manager;
    File &textfile;
     public:
    void do_processing( LineHandler linehandler );
        // do_processing creates Strings that
        // are passed to the client linehandler.
        // TextInput manages these Strings.
    int is_open() const;
```

```
TextInput( const char *path );
~TextInput();
    // All Strings created by
    // do_processing are destroyed
    // with the TextInput.
};
```

The client program provides the line handler function that does the per-line processing of the input file. The sequence of actions on the input file itself are simple, consisting of creating a `TextInput` object, checking to make sure the input is opened successfully, and then invoking `do_processing` with a line handler do the work.

```
extern void one_line_at_a_time( String & );
extern error( const char *, ... );

main() {
    TextInput text = "textfile";
    if( text.is_open() )
        text.do_processing( one_line_at_a_time );
    else
        error( "Cannot open text" );


}
```

Comments are used to note explicitly that the `TextInput` object takes responsibility for the management of the `String` objects it creates. Although such memory management responsibilities cannot be stated as part of the formal class declaration, they are, nonetheless, an essential part of the interface that must be understood for correct use of the class. A client must avoid creating pointers or references to `Strings` created by a `TextInput` object that persist in the program after the `TextInput` is deleted. Such pointers and references will be left dangling, referring to invalid objects. In order to retain a copy of a line of text beyond the lifetime of the `TextInput` object itself, the client must create its own copy of the `String` that is passed to the line handler.

Alternative policies could have been taken in the management of the `Strings` created by `TextInput`. One would be to have the `String` exist only for the duration of the call to the line handler. With this policy, `TextInput::do_processing` takes responsibility for managing the `String`, perhaps creating it as an automatic.

```
void
TextInput::do_processing( LineHandler linehandler ) {
    // ...
    {
        String line( linebuffer );
        linehandler( line );
    }
    //...
}
```

To retain a line of text beyond a single invocation of linehandler, the client makes its own copy. This makes the client responsible for the management of any lines it may want to save.

Another memory management policy would be to place the burden of deleting the strings on the client program. This policy trades the potential error of dangling references for that of memory leaks if the client overlooks its side of the responsibility for correct use of the class. The client responsibility should be highlighted both in the documentation and, if possible, in the interface design. One small way of doing this is to change the argument of the line handler function to a pointer, the usual way of accessing dynamically allocated objects. Of course, comments should note the memory management policy.

```
typedef void (*LineHandler)( String * );

class TextInput {
    //...
    void do_processing( LineHandler linehandler );
        // WARNING
        // do_processing creates Strings that
        // are passed to the client linehandler.
        // NOTE: The client is responsible for
        // deleting these Strings
    //...
};
```

When libraries provide comprehensive services at a high level of abstraction, information passed between the library and the client program may take the form of objects representing those abstractions. In this case, lifetime management of library interface objects becomes an issue that must be addressed in library design. The object management policies taken in the library design can affect the ease of use of the library, and even the likelihood of its correct use. These policies can also have implications for the efficiency of both the library implementation and the client program.

Class encapsulation provides a means for building library interfaces at a high level of abstraction. High level interfaces can greatly simplify client code that accesses the library services. However, while the abstract interface frees the client from burdensome details, responsibility for correctness and efficiency, traditionally left to the client program, now becomes an issue of library design and implementation.

8.2 Error Interfaces and Exceptions

A library may not always be able to provide the services requested by a client program. The causes of this inability may vary widely from user error to abnormal environment conditions. In any case, the client program must be able to detect such library failure and handle it appropriately. A library interface should include a way to report error or status information to the client in a suitable form. The suitability of an error or status interface depends on how severe and uncommon the error condition is.

The `stdio` functions provide status and error information through their return values. The function `fopen` returns a null pointer if it fails to open the requested file. The failure could be the result of a user error, such as providing an incorrect filename as an argument, or an environment condition, such as access restrictions on the file's directory. In either case, the failure can be considered so common as to be a part of the normal interface. A client is required to check the return value of `fopen` to see if it is valid before passing it to other `stdio` functions. A complete implementation of the `class File` encapsulation of `stdio` should provide a way of checking that the file is successfully opened.

```
inline int
File::valid() const { return f != 0; }
```

Another part of the `stdio` error interface is the global value `errno`. When an failure is flagged in a library function's return value, `errno` provides an integral code that gives more information about the cause of the failure. Although `errno` is part of the standard library, the use of a global variable is a poor error interface. It is not always clear what caused the global variable to be set, and client programmers commonly forget that `errno` and its set of code values are part of the library's interface. Global variables, in general, increase interference among multiple threads of execution in a single process, although `errno` itself may be implemented to behave safely in the standard library available in a multi-threaded environment.

The `TextInput` class of the previous section explicitly provides a member function `is_open` for a status query on the input file. Other queries could be added on the object state giving fine-grain status information of the sort provided by `errno`. `TextInput` may also go beyond the basic error checking of `stdio`, for example, checking that a file is indeed a text file, and not a binary file, before opening it. `TextInput::do_processing` should be implemented to be well behaved whether or not the correct conditions exist to process text. For example, it could simply do nothing if the input file is not open or is not text. As a high-level abstraction, it would be inappropriate for `TextInput` to terminate the client program for easily detectable conditions for which there is reasonable default behavior.

It is especially important for constructors and destructors to behave "reasonably" in the presence of an error condition, since it may be difficult or impossible for the user of a class to query status immediately after a constructor or destructor return. If a constructor is invoked within another constructor to initialize a member or a base class subobject, other member or base initializations may occur before control returns to the constructor body, where the status of the initializations may be checked. In a similar way, a destructor may invoke a base class or member destructor without being able to check for error until other base class or member destructors have completed execution.

Generally, it is a good policy to allow an object that has entered an error state to continue to be used without catastrophic error until its user has the opportunity to query its status. For example, we might consider re-writing the implementations of the `File` member functions to be more robust in the event that the constructor was unable to open the file.

```
inline int
File::flush() { return f ? fflush( f ) : 0; }
```

One extreme condition that `TextInput::do_processing` cannot handle well is the failure of dynamic memory allocation. The point of such failure is likely to be somewhere in the `String` library during the construction of an object to hold a line of input text. If such an exceptional failure prevents the normal completion of a library function, it is appropriate for the library simply to give up and let the client program decide what to do.

The C++ exception handling feature provides a mechanism for jumping out of the normal sequence of control flow, where an error condition has been detected, to an earlier context where the condition can reasonably be handled. To jump out of possibly deeply nested library function calls to the client, library code executes a `throw` expression. The `throw` expression general-ly indicates an object that describes the error condition that gave rise to the `throw`. The client application intercepts the thrown exception object by sur-rounding a code sequence with a `try` block. A `try` block has one or more exception handlers associated with it. Each handler consists of a `catch` clause followed by a block that handles the exception. The handler is execut-ed for an exception if the argument of the `throw` expression matches the de-claration in the `catch` clause.

For example, a library may have, as part of its error interface, a simple hierarchy representing different kinds of fatal errors.

```
class FatalError {
    char *msg;
  public:
    FatalError( const char *message );
    virtual void handleit()
        { log( msg ); exit( 1 ); }
};

class StackOverflow : public FatalError {
  public:
    StackOverflow()
        : FatalError( "stack overflow" ) {}
    void handleit() {
        if( ++count <= max ) {
            log( "stack overflow:  don't call so much" );
        else
            FatalError::handleit();
    }
  private:
    static long count;
    enum { max = 127 };
};
```

```
class MathErr : public FatalError {
  public:
    MathErr()
        : FatalError( "math error" ) {}
};

// ...
```

If the library code detects a condition from which it cannot recover, it throws the appropriate type of `FatalError` object.

```
if( cant_call )
    throw StackOverflow();
```

The client encloses code that calls the library, directly or indirectly, with a `try` block followed by a sequence of one or more exception handlers.

```
main() {
    while( continue_main_loop() ) {
        try {
            // ...
            something();
            // ...
        }
        catch( MathErr & ) {
            // we don't care about math errors...
            // loop again
        }
        catch( FatalError &fatalerr ) {
            fatalerr.handleit();
        }
        catch( OtherLibError &othererr ) {
            // ...
        }
        // etc.
    }
    exit( 0 );
}
```

When the `throw` expression in the library is executed, the execution stack is "unwound" until a `try` block is encountered with a `catch` clause that matches the type of the expression thrown. In this case, the `catch` clause for `FatalError` is matched because there is a predefined conversion from a `StackOverflow` object to a reference to its `FatalError` public base class. After execution of the handler, execution continues after the `try` block and its associated handlers unless the handler terminates the program or throws another exception.

Newer C++ implementations that support exception handling may have a standard exception type that is thrown when dynamic memory allocation fails. In such an environment, a client of `TextInput` can set up a handler for intelligent reporting of memory allocation failure. In the following, the environment exception type `xalloc` is caught in order to print out an error message before terminating the program.

```
if( text.is_open() )
    try {
        text.do_processing( one_line_at_a_time );
    }
    catch( xalloc &mem ) {
        error( "out of memory: processing incomplete" );
        exit( 1 );
    }
else
    error( "Cannot open text" );
```

A thrown exception has another important side effect in addition to unwinding the execution stack and executing the code of the matched handler: it activates any destructors for stack-based objects that are removed from the stack as a result of the unwinding.

Recall the `ResourceHandle` type of Chapter 7. Objects of types derived from `ResourceHandle` controlled the seizing and releasing of resources as a side effect of the execution of their constructors and destructors. If important resources, such as file handles, memory arenas, database locks, and processes are seized and released through stack resident resource handles, then those resources will be properly reclaimed as the stack is unwound during exception handling.

Exceptions are a useful programming and design feature, but, like multiple inheritance and operator overloading, are often overused. Exceptions should only be thrown for unrecoverable library failures since they may terminate the client program if uncaught. They are costly and may add considerable overhead to a program both for setting up exception handlers and when thrown. Library exceptions can give the client application a chance to roll back a failed operation and try something else or allow meaningful context information to be reported before the client gracefully terminates itself. However, exceptions should be used as exceptions and not as a means to report common status conditions.

8.3   Client Customizable Libraries

Libraries may provide services in the form of generic data structures or as general mechanisms for structuring control flow. Such library services must be customized to work with elements of the client program. Generic data structures are implemented in C++ with class templates. User customization of templates is accomplished through instantiation of the template for the types and constants specified by the client. Such generic data structures are discussed in Chapter 4 and are not discussed further here. When a library provides a control mechanism, customization is accomplished by means of client-implemented actions that are executed within the control framework.

The `TextInput` class discussed previously in this chapter demonstrates a technique by which a library may provide a client customizable control mechanism. The function `TextInput::do_processing` controls the iteration over each line in the input file. The specific action in each iteration is executed by the client-provided `LineHandler`. This technique is known as a "callback." The client registers a callback function with the library, and the library calls-back to the client function from within the control mechanism. The callback function is accessed through a pointer that is passed into the library as a parameter.

Inheritance can also be used to customize a library. The library services are provided in a set of base classes from which the client derives. An example of customization via inheritance is the task library shown in Chapter 6. The library provides a coroutine control mechanism in `class task`. Classes derived from `task` implement coroutines for the client program in their constructors.

Inheritance and virtual functions provide another mechanism for implementing callback functions. The technique is to provide default behavior in a virtual function provided in a library class. The client can use the default functionality or customize the behavior by deriving from the library class and providing an overriding virtual function.

For example, a button object in a graphical user interface, or GUI, can be implemented as a C++ class.

```
class Button : public Widget {
    //..
    virtual void action();
    virtual void show_help_message() const;
    //..
};
```

`Button` is assumed to be one class in a library that manages program control through a GUI. `Widget` is the base implementation of all the different kinds of GUI elements available in the library. The `Button` member function `action` is called by the library when a button object in the GUI is "pushed." Similarly, `show_help_message` is called in response to an event requesting help. In effect, `Button` specifies a protocol to which any type derived from `Button` must adhere. As with the `Protocol` type of Chapter 5, users of button types derived from `Button` need not be aware of the specifics of the derived types but can deal with them through the base class interface. To provide a program-specific action for the button, the client provides a derived class that overrides the `Button` default.

```
class ClientButton : public Button {
    //...
    void action();
    //...
};

void ClientButton::action() {
    // code to be executed when this type
    // of button is pushed.
    //...
}
```

`ClientButton` provides a customized `action`. The client application creates a customized button by using the derived type.

```
Button *bp = new ClientButton;
add_button_to_gui( bp );
```

The use of overriding virtual functions as a callback mechanism requires a programmer of client code to understand the library class well enough to define an appropriate derived class and also to implement the overriding virtual functions. To make this easy for the client programmer, the library interface should have a clear abstract design and a well defined and documented protocol. The inheritance mechanism also disallows the resetting of the callback action at run time. The following alternative button implementation uses a data member to store a pointer-to-function type callback.

```
typedef void (*Action_t)();
class SettableButton : public Widget {
    //..
    Action_t callback;
    void action() { if( callback ) callback(); }
    void set_action( Action_t afp ) { callback = afp; }
    //...
};
```

The client registers a callback function by calling `set_action` rather than defining a derived class. The `action` function could be implemented to execute a more intelligent default action when the callback is unset.

8.4 Library Extensibility

Software libraries are intended for use by many client programs. However, it is not feasible to anticipate and provide for the needs of all potential clients in a library implementation. Often a library provides a service that comes close to what is needed for an application without being exactly suitable. In these cases, it is helpful if the library is designed to be extensible so that support for the services needed by new clients can be added, while leaving the original library design and implementation intact. Inheritance can be used as a general mechanism for extending and specializing the functionality of a library design.

One aspect of the extensible design of an inheritance hierarchy is the appropriate layering of abstraction. Consider the abstract syntax tree node hierarchy of Chapter 5. This library provides a general abstraction of a binary operator, so it is easy to extend the library through inheritance to handle additional binary operators.

```
class And : public Binop {
  public:
    And( Node *l, Node *r ) : Binop(l,r) {}
    int eval() const
        { return left->eval() & right->eval(); }
};
```

To add a new binary operator, we simply augment the general abstraction with the specifics of the particular operator we are adding.

The library does not contain an abstraction of a unary operator, however, only a specific unary minus. Adding a new unary operator requires much more work, including the definition of general properties of unary operators (like destructor semantics) as well as properties of the specific operator being added.

```
class Uplus : public Node {
    Node *operand;
  public:
    Uplus( Node *o ) { operand = o; }
    ~Uplus() { delete operand; }
    int eval() const { return operand->eval(); }
};
```

Most of this class definition would not have been necessary if a general unary operator abstraction were present in the library. Not only does code need to be written that could otherwise be inherited, but the programmer needs to know more about the details of the library implementation in order to add the new class. For libraries with complex implementations, it may be difficult for programmers implementing extensions to get all the details correct. In general, one cannot foresee how a given library may be used or extended, and all levels of abstraction should be made explicit.

Another consideration in designing an inheritance hierarchy is the identification of general operations in a class's interface that could be customized or replaced. These operations should be declared as virtual functions to allow the addition of a derived class to create specialized variations of a library base implementation.

A library may provide services for variations of an abstraction, without there being any meaningful default behavior for the general abstraction. In this case, there are no appropriate virtual function implementations that can be provided in the base class. Indeed, it would be erroneous to instantiate such an abstraction as an actual object except as one of its specific variations. An *abstract class* can be used to make this kind of abstraction explicit.

Let us revisit our `Device` class of Chapter 6. All devices have the same interface, and should inherit from the `Device` base. Each kind of device must provide its own functionality for `read`, `write`, and `ioctl` since there is no meaningful default action for these operations. The `Device` class forces derived classes to provide their own versions of these virtual functions by declaring them to be pure. The declaration of pure virtual functions is what makes a class abstract, preventing objects of the class from being created. `Device` is further designed for use only by derived classes by providing only a `protected` constructor.

```
class Device {
  protected:
    Device();
  public:
    virtual ~Device();
    virtual int open( char *, int, int );
    virtual int close( int );
    virtual int read( int, char *, unsigned ) = 0;
    virtual int write( int, char *, unsigned ) = 0;
    virtual int ioctl( int, int, ... ) = 0;
};
```

If a class derived from `Device` fails to provide versions of these functions, it is itself an abstract class and cannot be instantiated as an object.

```
class Disk : public Device {
  public:
    Disk();
    ~Disk();
    int open( char *, int, int );
    int close( int );
    int read( int, char *, unsigned );
    int write( int, char *, unsigned );
    // a mistake: missing ioctl
};
//...
Device *dp = new Disk; // error!
```

An abstract class can be used in a library to declare explicitly a required protocol for object interfaces. Separating the interface protocol from the rest of the library implementation makes clear precisely what is required of new classes that are added to extend the library services.

Inheritance is not the only way to produce an extensible library. A library can also provide a set of atomic operations and a syntactic framework for extensibility. The standard C++ library for stream I/O, `iostream`, provides type-secure input/output that may be extended to handle user-defined types. The extension is accomplished by overloading the I/O operations for the new types. By contrast, the I/O facilities provided by the `stdio` library are not type-secure and not easily extended.

```
#include <stdio.h>

extern int age;
extern String name;
printf( "%s's age is %d\n", age, name ); // oops!
```

This code is "correct" C++ but will produce garbage on execution or possibly cause the program to bomb. The arguments `age` and `name` are in the wrong order for the format string, but the error is not detected because there is no type information available to tell the compiler that the format string expects first a `char *`, then an `int`. Even if we had gotten the arguments in the correct order, the print statement still would not work. The `printf` function expects a `char *` argument corresponding to the `%s` in the format string, but we have supplied a `String` argument. In the absence of type information, the C++ compiler does not know to supply the implicit conversion from `String` to `char *` (using `String::operator const char *`). We could supply the necessary type information

```
inline int
age_print( char *n, int a )
    { return printf( "%s's age is %d\n", n, a ); }
//...
age_print( name, age );
```

but this approach forces special-case handling of every printing situation.

A safer approach is provided by the `iostream` library. Note that `iostream` overloads the operators `<<` and `>>` to provide type-secure output and input respectively. The print statement above could be written as

```
cout << name << "'s age is " << age << "\n";
```

What follows is a simplified version of some of the features of the `iostream` library. We define an output stream class, including left shift operators, or "inserters," for inserting values onto the output stream.

```
typedef FILE *FP;

class ostream {
   FP f;
  public:
   ostream( FP fl ) : f( fl ) {}
   operator FP() { return f; }
   ostream &operator <<( const char * );
   ostream &operator <<( int );
   ostream &operator <<( long );
   ostream &operator <<( double );
};


ostream cout = stdout;
```

For our simplified version, we use the `stdio` library to implement the semantics of our shift operators.

```
ostream &
ostream::operator <<( const char *s ) {
   fprintf( f, "%s", s );
   return *this;
}
```

The definitions of the other instances of `ostream::operator <<` are similar. Note that each shift operator returns (a reference to) the `ostream` object for which it was invoked. This is what allows us to cascade several output operations into a single (noncomma) expression. Like most C++ operators, the shift operators are left associative, so the expression

```
cout << name << "'s age is " << age << "\n";
```

is parsed as

```
(((cout << name) << "'s age is ") << age) << "\n";
```

Since the `ostream` object `cout` is returned from each `operator <<`, this is equivalent to

```
cout << name;
cout << "'s age is ";
cout << age;
cout << "\n";
```

but is far easier to read.

An input stream can be created in a similar fashion, defining right shift operators, or "extractors," for extracting values from the input stream.

```
class istream {
    FP f;
  public:
    istream( FP fl ) : f(fl) {}
    operator FP() { return f; }
    istream &operator >>( char * );
    istream &operator >>( int & );
    istream &operator >>( long & );
    istream &operator >>( double & );
    int gchar(); // get one char
};

istream &
istream::operator >>( long &l ) {
    fscanf( f, "%ld", &l );
    return *this;
}

istream cin = stdin;

cout << "Your age and name: ";
int age;
char nm[32];
cin >> age >> nm;
```

The classes `ostream` and `istream` form the basis of an extensible I/O library by defining I/O operations for C++'s predefined types and by defining, by example, a syntax for input and output operations. This framework can be extended to user-defined types by defining additional overloaded shift operators. For example, we may want to perform input and output of complex numbers.

```
class complex {
    double re, im;
  public:
    friend ostream &
    operator <<( ostream &, const complex & );
    friend istream &
    operator >>( istream &, complex & );
    // ...
};
```

The friend declarations are necessary in this case to allow the shift operators access to the private representation of the complex number. The shift operators for `complex` I/O are defined in terms of the shift operators for the predefined types, just as `complex` itself is defined in terms of predefined types.

```
ostream &
operator <<( ostream &out, const complex &c ) {
    out << "(" << c.re << "," << c.im << ")";
    return out;
}

istream &
operator >>( istream &in, complex &c ) {
    in >> ws; // See Exercise 8-7.
    if( in.gchar() != '(' ) error();
    in >> c.re;
    in >> ws;
    if( in.gchar() != ',' ) error();
    in >> c.im;
    in >> ws;
    if( in.gchar() != ')' ) error();
    return in;
}
```

Note that the `<<` operator outputs a complex number in a format that is acceptable to the `>>` operator for input.

How about output of a more complex user-defined type, such as an abstract syntax tree? We would like to be able to write code like

```
extern Node *np;
cout << "The expression is: " << np;
```

to print a fully parenthesized infix representation of the tree whose root is referred to by np.

We approach the problem by first adding a virtual printing capability to the abstract syntax tree node hierarchy.

```
class Node {
    //...
    virtual void print( ostream & ) const = 0;
};

class Binop : public Node {
    //...
    virtual void print_op( ostream & ) const = 0;
    void print( ostream &out ) const {
        out << "(";
        left->print( out );
        print_op( out );
        right->print( out );
        out << ")";
    }
};

class Plus : public Binop {
    //...
    void print_op( ostream &out ) const { out << "+"; }
};

class Int : public Node {
    //...
    void print( ostream &out ) const { out << value; }
};

// etc. ...
```

The operation of the virtual print routines is similar to that of the virtual eval routines and the virtual destructors already present in the abstract syntax tree node hierarchy. The routines recursively print the abstract syntax tree, calling the proper print routine based on the root node type of each subtree.

All that remains is to hook these member `print` routines up to the existing `iostream` library.

```
ostream &
operator <<( ostream &out, const Node *np ) {
    np->print( out );
    return out;
}
```

In an earlier example, we requested user input and then waited for a response.

```
cout << "Your age and name: ";
```

Unfortunately, this may not work in the way we intend. If the output stream `cout` is buffered, the message to the user may wait indefinitely for the output buffer to fill before it is actually written. To get the correct behavior we should flush the `cout` buffer to ensure that the message is actually written.

```
cout << "Your age and name: ";
flush( cout );
```

Control signals of this kind interspersed with input and output operations adversely affect the readability of the code, however, and distract both the coder and reader from the program logic. We would prefer to write

```
cout << "Your age and name: " << flush;
```

We accomplish this with applicators and manipulators. A manipulator is a value in an expression that causes a side effect that is not strictly related to the major purpose of the expression. Typically, these values are function addresses.

```
ostream &flush( ostream & );
```

To allow such function addresses to be used in output expressions, we define an applicator that applies its function (pointer) argument to the output stream and returns the output stream.

```
typedef ostream & (*Manip) (ostream&);

inline ostream &
operator <<( ostream &out, Manip f )
    { return f( out ); }
```

This applicator allows any manipulator of type `Manip` to be used in an output shift expression. Other applicators can be defined for manipulators with different types.

```
typedef int (*Manip2) (FILE *);

inline ostream &
operator <<( ostream &out, Manip2 f ) {
    f( out );
    return out;
}

extern int close( FILE * );

cout << "So long..." << flush << close;
```

It is frequently useful to allow parameterized manipulators. For instance, we may want to set various data transmission characteristics of an output stream to given argument values.

```
enum { odd, even, none };
enum { slow = 1200, lagom = 4800, fast = 9600 };

cout<<speed(fast)<<parity(none)<<"login: "<<flush;
```

In this case, the manipulator values are class objects that contain pairs of values: a function address and an integer argument value.

```
struct act_rec {
    void (*fp) (FILE *, int);
    int arg;
    act_rec( void (*f) (FILE *, int), int a )
        : fp(f), arg(a) {}
};
```

Note that `speed` and `parity` are functions that return `act_rec`s.

```
inline act_rec
speed( int baudr ) {
    extern void set_speed( FILE *, int );
    return act_rec( set_speed, baudr );
}
```

Finally, we define an applicator that applies an `act_rec` to an `ostream`.

```
inline ostream &
operator <<( ostream &out, act_rec m ) {
    m.fp( out, m.arg );
    return out;
}
```

8.5 Exercises

Exercise 8-1. †Design a message buffer type, similar in use to the `ostream` type of this chapter, that allows a user to construct a message incrementally. Provide insertion operators for character strings, numeric types, characters, and other message buffers, and a way to extract the character string thus constructed. Consider the following points in your design: What other operations besides insertion would be useful for a message buffer type? Who obtains and manages the memory for the buffer that contains the message under construction: the message buffer type or the user? When is this memory freed? What error conditions can arise, and how should the user of your type be informed of them? □

Exercise 8-2. †Modify your implementation of the message buffer type of the previous exercise so that users can derive message buffer types that behave differently on buffer overflow. □

Exercise 8-3. Modify your implementation of the message buffer type of the previous two exercises to employ customized memory management for its buffers. Disallow user allocation of objects of the type on the heap. □

Exercise 8-4. Examine the date and time facilities provided in your local environment. Are they simple and easy to use? Are they safe for multi-threaded access? Are error conditions clearly specified and easily detectable? Is code that uses the facilities easily ported to a different environment? Design a type that encapsulates these facilities so as to provide the above benefits. □

Exercise 8-5. Develop a library to make C++ into an application-oriented language for vector and matrix arithmetic. □

Exercise 8-6. Design a library for a relational database algebra. Implement two interfaces to the database operators: one that uses infix operators, and another that uses function call syntax. (Hint: How will you represent properties for searches, as abstract syntax trees? What is the difference between database access software and a programming language interpreter?) Design control structures to extend your relational algebra to a relational calculus. □

Exercise 8-7. Write an `istream` manipulator and applicator that consumes (discards) white space.

```
cin >> ws;
```

Write an `ostream` manipulator that inserts a newline and flushes the ostream buffer.

```
cout << endl;
```

□

Exercise 8-8. †Write a manipulator and applicator for class `complex` to do rounding for additions:

```
extern complex a, b, c, d;
d = a + b + round + c + round;
```

Write an analogous manipulator that performs the same operation for (predefined) integer expressions. □

Exercise 8-9. Write an applicator that applies manipulators of type `void(*)(char *)` to arguments of type `char *`. □

Exercise 8-10. Modify the `String` class of Chapter 4 to allow the application of manipulators of type `void (*)(String &)` and `void (*)(char *)` in `String` expressions. □

Exercise 8-11. †Write an inserter for the `SortedCollection` type of Chapter 4. Do not change the implementation or interface of the `SortedCollection`. □

Exercise 8-12. Write an extractor for abstract syntax trees corresponding to the inserter described in this chapter. You cannot assume the input is fully parenthesized, however. (Hint: What is the difference between a parser for the calculator language of Chapter 5 and this extractor?) □

Exercise 8-13. Given the definition of `iostream` in this chapter, explain why the expression `cfile >> first << replacement` will not compile. Redesign the implementation of `iostream` so that mixed I/O expressions like this are legal. □

Exercise 8-14. Are `<<` and `>>` good choices for the `streamio` insertion and extraction operators? Why or why not? What other operator(s) would be good choices? Why would `->` be a bad choice? Why would `+=` be a bad choice? □

Exercise 8-15. Show how the use of inheritance to customize class types can be used to fix library bugs without altering the library source. Use this technique to circumvent the environment-dependent order of evaluation of the operands of binary abstract syntax tree nodes in the `eval` function, as pointed out in the solution to Exercise 5-4. □

Exercise 8-16. †Often a library requires initialization before use. Design a scheme that will ensure that a library is initialized (once) in any application in which it is included. □

Exercise 8-17. Some customizable libraries are designed to be ''application frameworks,'' that is, blank applications that are customized to produced a family of real applications.

Refer to Exercise 6-5. Design an application framework for applications that are modeled as a sequence of state transitions. Implement an airline reservation system, a lexical analyzer for C++, and the finite state automaton abstract data type of Exercise 4-17 by using inheritance to customize your framework. □

Exercise 8-18. Consider any low-level interface to an ISAM database package. The major concepts behind the database include files, indexes, keys, properties, sequential access, and random access. How does the low-level interface represent these concepts? How easy to learn and use is the interface, and how likely is it that it may be accidentally misused? Design a C++ interface to the ISAM package that makes these concepts clearer and less prone to error. □

Exercise 8-19. In the previous exercise, were you able to represent all aspects of the original interface in your C++ version, or were there aspects of the original interface that were too low-level to fit within your conceptual framework? Design a mechanism that maintains a clean conceptual framework while allowing access to low-level features of the original interface if the need arises. □

Exercise 8-20. Consider the function template for `input` of Section 2.6. Can this template be instantiated with a `complex`? How would the use of stream input and output help? □

Exercise 1-2.

```
a       // int
b       // int *
*b      // int
c       // int *
*c      // int
d[2]    // int *
*d      // int *
**d     // int
c[-2]   // int
c-2     // int *
*(c-2)  // int
&c      // int **
```

□

Exercise 1-3.

```
c = cc;         // legal
cc = c;         // illegal
pcc = &c;       // legal
pcc = &cc;      // legal
pc = &c;        // legal
pc = &cc;       // illegal
pc = pcc;       // illegal
pc = cpc;       // legal
pc = cpcc;      // illegal
cpc = pc;       // illegal
*cpc = *pc;     // legal
```

```
pc = *pcpc;      // legal
**pcpc = *pc;    // legal
*pc = **pcpc;    // legal
```

☐

Exercise 2-4.

```
char *
get_token( char *&s, char *ws = " \t\n" ) {
   char *p;
   do
      for( p = ws; *p && *s != *p; p++ );
   while( *p ? *s++ : 0 );
   char *ret = s;
   do
      for( p = ws; *p && *s != *p; p++ );
   while( *p ? 0 : *s ? s++ : 0 );
   return ret;
}

int strlen( char *s ) {
   char *t = get_token( s, "" );
   return s-t;
}
```

☐

Exercise 3-1. A union is used to get at the bit representation of the double argument.

```
void
bitprint( double val ) {
   static int nbitsinchar = 0;
   if( !nbitsinchar ) {
      // calculate number of bits in a char
      for( unsigned char c = 1; c; c <<= 1 )
         nbitsinchar++;
   }
   union {
      double d;
      unsigned char a[ sizeof(double) ];
   };
   d = val;
```

```
for( int i = 0; i < sizeof(double); i++ ) {
    unsigned c = a[i];
    for( int j = nbitsinchar; j; j-- )
        if( c & ( 1 << j ) )
            printf("1");
        else
            printf("0");
}
```

☐

Exercise 3-2. We use a circular list to implement the abstract list type.

```
class PtrList {
    public:
    PtrList()
        : last( 0 ) {}
    ~PtrList();
    void prepend( void * );
    void append( void * );
    void *pop_front();
    int empty() const;
    private:
    struct El {
        void *p;
        El *next;
    } *last;  // circular
};

void
PtrList::prepend( void *v ) {
    El *el = new El;
    el->p = v;
    if( last ) {
        el->next = last->next;
        last->next = el;
    }
    else
        last = el->next = el;
}
```

```
typedef int (*Pred)( T );

class Ctl {
  public:
    Ctl( const SortedCollection &sc )
        : c( sc ), i( 0 ) {}
    ~Ctl()
        {}
    void reset()
        { i = 0; }
    int done() const
        { return i >= c.free; }
    void next()
        { i++; }
    void next( Pred );
    T get() const
        { return c.ary[i]; }
  private:
    const SortedCollection &c;
    int i;
};

void
Ctl::next( Pred p ) {
    while( ++i < c.free )
        if( p( c.ary[i] ) )
            break;
}
```

Use of Ctl is straightforward.

```
int odd( int i ) { return i & 1; }
//...
for( Ctl ctl = c; !ctl.done(); ctl.next() )
    // ...
ctl.reset()
ctl.next( odd );
// ...
```

□

Exercise 4-20.

```
typedef void (*Manip)( T & );

class Tree {
  public:
    Tree()
        : root( 0 ) {}
    ~Tree()
        { delete root; }
    int insert( T );
    void inorder_apply( Manip m )
        { if( root ) root->apply( m ); }
  private:
    class Node {
      public:
        Node *left, *right;
        T el;
        Node( T e )
            : left( 0 ), right( 0 ), el( e ) {}
        ~Node();
        int insert( T );
        void apply( Manip );
    } *root;
    friend class Inorder;  // for next exercise
};

int
Tree::insert( T el ) {
    if( root )
        return root->insert( el );
    root = new Node( el );
    return 1;
}

int
Tree::Node::insert( T arg ) {
    if( arg == el )
        return 0;
```

```
        if( arg < el )
            if( left )
                return left->insert( arg );
            else {
                left = new Node( arg );
                return 1;
            }
        if( right )
            return right->insert( arg );
        right = new Node( arg );
        return 1;
    }

    void
    Tree::Node::apply( Manip m ) {
        if( left )
            left->apply( m );
        m( el );
        if( right )
            right->apply( m );
    }
```

☐

Exercise 4-21. The inorder control abstraction must essentially behave like
the inorder apply function of the previous exercise, but must return after
visiting each node, and pick up again where it left off. Our approach is to
have the control abstraction simulate a recursive inorder function by
maintaining a stack of "function activations."

```
    class Inorder {
      public:
        Inorder( const Tree &t )
            : top( t.root ? new ActRec( t.root, 0 ) : 0 )
            { next(); }
        ~Inorder();
        int done() const
            { return top == 0; }
        void next();
        T get() const
            { return top->root->el; }
```

```
    private:
      class ActRec {   // simulated activation record
        public:
          Tree::Node *root;   // local data
          enum { LEFT, VISIT, RIGHT, RETURN } pc;
          ActRec *prev;     // previous invocation
          ActRec( Tree::Node *r, ActRec *p )
              : root( r ), pc( LEFT ), prev( p ) {}
      } *top;    // top of activation stack
};
```

The next function branches to the correct section of code by examining the
program counter, and pushes or pops activation records as appropriate. The
algorithm is the same as that used in Tree::Node::apply.

```
    void
    Inorder::next() {
        while( top )
            switch( top->pc ) {
            case ActRec::LEFT:
                top->pc = ActRec::VISIT;
                if( top->root->left )
                    top = new ActRec( top->root->left, top );
                break;
            case ActRec::VISIT:
                top->pc = ActRec::RIGHT;
                return;
            case ActRec::RIGHT:
                top->pc = ActRec::RETURN;
                if( top->root->right )
                    top = new ActRec( top->root->right, top );
                break;
            case ActRec::RETURN:
                ActRec *tmp = top;
                top = top->prev;
                delete tmp;
                break;
            }
    }
```

□

Exercise 4-26. An associative array maps index values to elements of the array. According to this definition, a standard C++ array is associative: it maps integers to array elements. Another example of an associative array is a compiler symbol table because it maps identifiers to their attributes. Our associative array is going to map Strings to Strings, so both the index and element type are String.

```
typedef String I;
typedef String E;
```

To implement the mapping from String to String, we create an associative array class and overload the [] operator to allow us to index our associative array as if it were a regular array.

```
class Pair {
    I index;
    E el;
    Pair *next;
    friend class Aary;
};

class Aary {
  public:
    Aary()
        { elems = 0; }
    ~Aary();
    E &operator[]( I );
  private:
    Pair *elems;
    Aary( Aary & );
    void operator =( Aary & );
};
```

For this implementation, our array is just a list of index, element pairs. The index operator performs a linear search of the list each time the associative array is indexed. This is appropriate for arrays with few indices, but for large arrays a more efficient search method is indicated.

```
E &
Aary::operator[]( I i ) {
    for( Pair *p = elems; p; p = p->next )
        if( p->index == i )
            return p->el;
    p = new Pair;
    p->index = i;
    p->next = elems;
    elems = p;
    return p->el;
}
```

Note that `operator[]` creates an element on access if it does not exist already. Now we can declare and use our dictionary type.

```
Aary dict;
dict["cat"] = "meow";
dict["dog"] = "moo";
dict["cow"] = "woof";
dict["sheep"] = "baa";
dict["dog"] = dict["cow"];
dict["cow"] = "moo";
```

Our implementation imposes very few constraints on the index and element types. The index type must have the operators == and = defined, and the element type must have the operator = defined. In addition, both types must be able to be declared without an initializer or to have a default initializer.

We take advantage of these observations and make our type generic through use of a class template.

```
template <class I, class E> Aary;

template <class I, class E>
class Pair {
    I index;
    E el;
    Pair *next;
    friend class Aary<I,E>;
};
```

```
template <class I, class E>
class Aary {
  public:
    Aary()
        { elems = 0; }
    ~Aary();
    E &operator[]( I );
  private:
    Pair<I,E> *elems;
    Aary( Aary & );
    void operator =( Aary & );
};
```

Now we can instantiate versions of our generic type and declare objects of the instantiated type.

We can instantiate our original dictionary type by using `String` as both the index and element type.

```
typedef Aary<String,String> Dictionary;
Dictionary dict;
```

Other instantiations might include a compiler symbol table

```
Aary<String,NameInfo> symbol_table;
```

or a very large, sparse array with integer indicies.

```
typedef Aary<long,Type> LargeAry;
LargeAry a;
Type x, y, z;
a[0] = x;
a[1000000000] = y;
a[2000000000] = z;
```

Notice that we cannot instantiate an associative array type whose elements are associative arrays.

```
Aary<String,Dictionary> library; // error!
```

Why? Re-write the `Aary` template to remove this restriction. □

Exercise 4-27. We use the old trick of using exclusive OR to encode the bits for both the previous and next link pointers into a single pointer. We can recover the address of the previous element from the encoding if we have the address of the next element and conversely.

```
encoded = previous ^ next;
next == encoded ^ previous;
previous == encoded ^ next;
```

To traverse the list in either direction, all we need are unencoded addresses for the head and tail of the list.

```
typedef int Etype;
typedef int Bits;

class ListEl {
    ListEl *ptr;
    Etype el;
    friend class List;
    friend class Iter;
    friend void paste( ListEl *&, ListEl *&, Etype );
};

class List {
    ListEl *hd, *tl;
  public:
    List() { hd = tl = 0; }
    friend List &operator +( List &, Etype );
    friend List &operator +=( Etype, List & );
    ListEl *head() { return hd; }
    ListEl *tail() { return tl; }
    friend class Iter;
};
```

We overload the += operator to add an element at the head of the list, and the + operator to add an element to the end of the list.

```
List &
operator +( List &lst, Etype e ) {
    paste( lst.tl, lst.hd, e );
    return lst;
}

List &
operator +=( Etype e, List &lst ) {
    paste( lst.hd, lst.tl, e );
    return lst;
}
```

```
void
paste( ListEl *&front, ListEl *&back, Etype e ) {
    ListEl *tmp = new ListEl;
    tmp->el = e;
    if( !front )
        back = front = tmp;
    else if( back == front ) {
        back->ptr = front = tmp;
        tmp->ptr = back;
    }
    else {
        tmp->ptr = front;
        front->ptr =
            (ListEl *)(Bits(front->ptr) ^ Bits(tmp));
        front = tmp;
    }
}
```

An iterator object is initialized with the end of the list at which the traversal is to start.

```
class Iter {
    ListEl *prev, *curr;
  public:
    Iter( ListEl *start ) { prev = 0; curr = start; }
    Etype *operator ()();
};

Etype *
Iter::operator ()() {
    if( !curr )
        return 0;
    ListEl *tmp = curr;
    curr = (ListEl *)(Bits(curr->ptr) ^ Bits(prev));
    prev = tmp;
    return &tmp->el;
}
```

Now we can create lists and traverse them in either direction.

```
typedef int Etype;
#include "list.h"

main() {
    int *ip;
    List ints;
    1 += 2 += 3 += ints + 4 + 5 + 6;

    Iter forw = ints.head();
    while( ip = forw() )
       printf( "%d ", *ip );

    Iter backw = ints.tail();
    while( ip = backw() )
       printf( "%d ", *ip );
}
```

Although the integers in the list are in ascending order, they are added to the list in the order 4, 5, 6, 3, 2, 1. Why? What do you think about our use of the += operator for adding elements to the head of the list? Is this a good idea?

One important aspect of this solution to the problem is that the encoded representation of the forward and backward links is hidden from users of the list. When we come to our senses later and decide to use separate forward and backward link pointers, we can make the change without affecting the code that uses the list. □

Exercise 5-4. First, we define an identifier node type and a symbol table to map identifiers to values. Since there are no declarations in our calculator language, we create a symbol table entry for a name the first time its identifier is used.

```
class Id : public Node {
  public:
    Id( const char *nm )
       : entry( look( nm ) ) {}
    int set( int i )
       { return entry->value = i; }
    int eval() const
       { return entry->value; }
```

```
    private:
      class Nament {
          friend class Id;
          char *name;
          int value;
          Nament *next;
          Nament( const char *nm, Nament *n )
              : name( strcpy( new char[ strlen(nm)+1 ], nm ) ),
                value( 0 ), next( n ) {}
      };
      static Nament *symtab;
      Nament *entry;
      Nament *look( const char * );
  };

  Id::Nament *
  Id::look( const char *nm ) {
      for( Nament *p = symtab; p; p = p->next )
          if( strcmp( p->name, nm ) == 0 )
              return p;
      return symtab = new Nament( nm, symtab );
  }
```

Next, we define an assignment node type.

```
  class Assign : public Binop {
    public:
      Assign( Id *t, Node *e )
          : Binop( t, e ) {}
      int eval() const
          { return ((Id *)left)->set( right->eval() ); }
  };
```

Note that we have to cast the `left` pointer in order to invoke `Id::set` in `Assign::eval`. Why? We could avoid the cast by declaring `set` to be a virtual member function in `Node`. Why is this a bad idea?

Ordinarily, we should not have to change the implementations of the other abstract syntax tree node types to accommodate the addition of the assignment operator. We made an *implicit* assumption in the implementation of the other binary operators, however, that evaluation order does not matter. Let us look at the implementation of `Plus::eval`.

```
int
Plus::eval() const
    { return left->eval() + right->eval(); }
```

Recall that C++ does not completely define the evaluation order of expressions. Therefore, we cannot say whether the left or the right subtree of the addition will be evaluated first. This is generally all right if the expression being evaluated has no side effects, but assignment statements do have side effects. Consider the effect of evaluating the right subtree of an addition before the left subtree in the following expression: `(id = 12) + id`. A more portable implementation of `Plus::eval` would be

```
int
Plus::eval() const {
    int l = left->eval();
    return l + right->eval();
}
```

An implementation of an interactive calculator that uses our abstract syntax tree hierarchy is given below.

```c++
#include <stdio.h>
#include <string.h>
#include <ctype.h>
#include "Nodes.h"

class Lex {  // generic lexical analyser interface
  public:
    Lex( size_t lexeme_size = 81 )
        : str( new char[ lexeme_size ] ) {}
    virtual ~Lex()
        { delete [] str; }
    virtual void scan() = 0;
    int token()
        { return tok; }
    const char *lexeme()
        { return str; }
  protected:
    int tok;
    char *str;
};

class CharLex : public Lex { // reads char stream
  protected:
    // unless overridden, reads from stdin
    virtual int nextchar()
        { return getchar(); }
    virtual void unnextchar( char c )
        { ungetc( c, stdin ); }
};

class ExprLex : public CharLex {// lex for exprs
  public:
    void scan();
};
```

```
enum { ID = 257, INT, EOLN, BAD };

/*
    Scanner:  return the next token in the input stream.
        attributes for integer constants and identifiers
        available until next invocation
*/
void
ExprLex::scan() {
    int c;
    while( 1 )
        switch( c = nextchar() ) {
        case '+': case '-':
        case '*': case '/':
        case '(': case ')':
        case '=':
            tok = c;
            return;
        case ' ': case '\t':
            continue;
        case '\n':
            tok = EOLN;
            return;
        default:
            if( isdigit( c ) ) {
                char *s = str;
                do
                    *s++ = c;
                while( isdigit( c = nextchar() ) );
                *s = '\0';
                unnextchar( c );
                tok = INT;
                return;
            }
```

```
        if( isalpha( c ) ) {
            char *s = str;
            do
                *s++ = c;
            while( isalnum(c = nextchar()) );
            *s = '\0';
            unnextchar( c );
            tok = ID;
            return;
        }
        tok = BAD;
        return;
    }
}

class Parser {   // generic parser interface
  public:
    Parser( Lex *lp )
        : lex( lp ) {}
    virtual ~Parser()
        { delete lex; }
    virtual Node *parse() = 0;
  protected:
    void scan()
        { lex->scan(); }
    int token()
        { return lex->token(); }
    const char *lexeme()
        { return lex->lexeme(); }
  private:
    Lex *lex;
};
```

```
/*
    Predictive parser for a simple expression grammar:

        E --> T {(+|-)T}
        T --> F {(*|/)F}
        F --> ID | INT | ( E ) | ID = E | -F
*/
class ExprParser : public Parser {
  public :
    ExprParser( Lex *lp )
        : Parser( lp ) {}
    ~ExprParser()
        {}
    Node *parse();
  private:
    Node *e();
    Node *t();
    Node *f();
    void error();
};

Node *
ExprParser::parse() {
    scan();
    Node *ast = e();
    if( token() != EOLN )
        error();
    return ast;
}

void
ExprParser::error() {
    printf( "ERROR!!!\n" );
    exit( 255 );
}
```

```
Node *
ExprParser::e() {
    Node *root = t();
    while( 1 )
        switch( token() ) {
        case '+':
            scan();
            root = new Plus( root, t() );
            break;
        case '-':
            scan();
            root = new Minus( root, t() );
            break;
        default:
            return root;
        }
}

Node *
ExprParser::f() {
    Node *root;
    switch( token() ) {
    case ID:
        root = new Id( lexeme() );
        scan();
        if( token() == '=' ) {
            scan();
            root = new Assign( (Id *)root, e() );
        }
        return root;
    case INT:
        root = new Int( atoi( lexeme() ) );
        scan();
        return root;
    case '(':
        scan();
        root = e();
        if( token() != ')' )
            error();
        scan();
        return root;
```

```
            case '-':
                scan();
                return new Uminus( f() );
            default:
                error();
            }
    }


Node *
ExprParser::t() {
    Node *root = f();
    while( 1 )
        switch( token() ) {
        case '*':
            scan();
            root = new Times( root, f() );
            break;
        case '/':
            scan();
            root = new Div( root, f() );
            break;
        default:
            return root;
        }
}


/*
    Driver:  initialize, loop while no error.
*/
main() {
    Parser *parser = new ExprParser( new ExprLex );
    while( 1 ) {
        printf( "Enter an expression:   " );
        Node *root = parser->parse();
        if( root ) {
            printf( "Result:  %d\n", root->eval() );
            delete root;
        }
    }
    delete parser;
}
```

□

Exercise 5-8. We first create a base class similar to the original list of `void *`s of Exercise 3-2.

```
class PtrListBase {
    protected:
    PtrListBase();
    ~PtrListBase();
    void prepend( void * );
    void append( void * );
    void *pop_front();
    int empty() const;
    private:
    // ...
};
```

We then create a class template whose instantiations simply maintain type safety. The type conversions provided by the inline functions (typically) operate entirely at compile time and cause no code to be generated.

```
template <class T>
class PtrList : private PtrListBase {
    public:
    PtrList()
        {}
    ~PtrList()
        {}
    void prepend( T *t )
        { PtrListBase::prepend( t ); }
    void append( T *t )
        { PtrListBase::append( t ); }
    T *pop_front()
        { return (T *) PtrListBase::pop_front(); }
    int empty() const
        { return PtrListBase::empty(); }
};
```

☐

Exercise 5-10. c) First we modify the constructor and destructor for `Node`, the root class of our abstract syntax tree hierarchy, to keep track of the number of nodes allocated. It is sufficient to modify only the constructor and destructor for `Node` because these are invoked any time a constructor or destructor for any class derived from `Node` is invoked.

```
class Node {
  protected:
   Node()
       { count++; }
  public:
    ~Node()
        { count--; }
    virtual int eval();
    static long num_nodes()
        { return count; }
  private:
    static long count;
};
```

The count static data member is defined elsewhere.

```
long Node::count = 0;
```

Now we can derive a new monitor type that monitors the number of nodes.

```
class Nalloc : public Monitor {
   long max_nodes;
  public:
   double get_display_value() {
       return Node::num_nodes() > max_nodes
              ? max_nodes
              : Node::num_nodes();
   }
   Nalloc( long max = 1000 ) :
       Monitor( "Nodes", 0, max, 0.5 ),
       max_nodes( max ) {}
};
```

☐

Exercise 5-18. One possible view of a "virtual" constructor would be a member function that returns a copy of its object.

```
class Thing {
  public:
   virtual Thing *copy() = 0;
   virtual Thing *clone() = 0;
   // ...
};
```

```
class OneThing : public Thing {
  public:
    Thing *copy();
    Thing *clone();
    OneThing();
    OneThing( const OneThing & );
    // ...
};

class Another : public Thing {
  public:
    Another( int = 1, int = 2 );
    Thing *copy();
    Thing *clone();
    // ...
  private:
    Another( const Another & );
    // ...
};
```

The implementations of the `copy` and `clone` operations are straightforward.

```
Thing *
OneThing::copy()
    { return new OneThing(); }

Thing *
OneThing::clone()
    { return new OneThing( *this ); }
```

□

Exercise 5-22. A literal such as 256 was not used in order to ease maintenance of the class; since the literal value would appear at several locations in the implementation of the class, it is more convenient and safer to be able to change the size of the hash table at a single point.

A `#define` was not used because it cannot be scoped inside the class, even with the use of `#undef`, without engendering maintenance difficulties far in excess of simply using a literal as above.

A constant data member cannot be used because its value is not known at compile time. The compiler must know the size of the array when the class is compiled, but the value of a data member, whether static or non-static, is not known until runtime.

The scoped enumerator is the only language feature available that provides a compile time constant that is scoped within the class and is easy to maintain. □

Exercise 6-4. Simulation with central control of multiple airports:

```
#include <stdio.h>
#include "task.h"

class Airport;

class Plane : public object {
    static int fltcount;
    long start;
    int fltno;
    Airport *origin;
    Airport *destination;
  public:
    Plane( Airport *o, Airport *d ) {
        fltno = ++fltcount;
        origin = o;
        destination = d;
    }
    long howlong() { return sched::get_clock() - start; }
    void set() { start = sched::get_clock(); }
    int flt() { return fltno; }
    Airport *to() { return destination; }
    Airport *from() { return origin; }
    void reschedule();
};

class PlaneQ {
    qhead *head;
    qtail *tail;
```

```
  public:
    PlaneQ() {  head = new qhead( ZMODE, 50 );
              tail = head->tail();}
    void put( Plane *p ) { p->set();
              tail->put( (object*)p );}
    Plane *get() { return (Plane *)head->get(); }
    int isroom() { return tail->rdspace(); }
    int notempty() { return head->rdcount(); }
};

class AirControl : public task  {
    PlaneQ  *landing, *inair, *incoming, *outgoing;
    PlaneQ  *incircling, *outcircling;
    int ok_take_off;
  public:
    AirControl( PlaneQ*, PlaneQ*, PlaneQ*, PlaneQ* );
    ~AirControl();
    int tok() { return ok_take_off; }
};

class GroundControl : public task {
    PlaneQ *takingoff, *onground;
  public:
    GroundControl( PlaneQ*, PlaneQ* );
};

class Airport : public task {
    PlaneQ  *takingoff, *landing, *inair,
        *onground, *incoming, *outgoing;
    AirControl *acontrol;
    GroundControl *gcontrol;
    const int index;
    char * const nm;
  public:
    Airport( PlaneQ *, PlaneQ*, int, char* );
    ~Airport();
    char *name() { return nm; }
    friend CentralControl;
};
```

```
class CentralControl : public task {
    static nairports;
    static Airport **airports;
    static urand *acity;
  public:
    CentralControl();
    ~CentralControl();
    friend Airport *pickacity() {
        return CentralControl::
            airports[CentralControl::acity->draw()];}
};

Airport::Airport( PlaneQ *in, PlaneQ *out,
            int i, char *id ) :
    incoming(in), outgoing(out), index(i), nm(id) {

    takingoff = new PlaneQ;
    inair = new PlaneQ;
    landing = new PlaneQ;
    onground = new PlaneQ;
    acontrol = new AirControl( landing, inair,
                incoming, outgoing );
    gcontrol = new GroundControl( takingoff,onground);
    Plane *tp=0, *lp=0; // waiting planes
    int maxwait = 30;
    for(;;){
        delay( 10 );
        if( !lp ) lp = landing->get();
        if( !tp && acontrol->tok() ) tp = takingoff->get();
        if( lp ){
            if( onground->isroom() ) {
                printf("flight %d from %s landing at %s\n",
                    lp->flt(), lp->from()->name(), name());
                onground->put( lp );
                lp = 0;
            }
            else if( lp->howlong() > maxwait ) {
                printf("flight %d crash landing at %s!\n",
                    lp->flt(), name());
                delete lp;
                lp = 0;
```

```
        } else
            printf("flight %d landing at %s delayed\n",
                lp->flt(), name());
    }
    if( tp ) {
        if( inair->isroom() ) {
            printf("flight %d from %s to %s taking off\n",
                tp->flt(), name(), tp->to()->name());
            inair->put( tp );
            tp = 0;
        } else
            printf("flight %d take off from %s delayed\n",
                lp ->flt(), name() );
        }
    } // end for(;;)
}

AirControl::AirControl( PlaneQ *land, PlaneQ *ina,
            PlaneQ *income, PlaneQ *outgo) :
    landing(land), inair(ina),
            incoming(income), outgoing(outgo) {
    incircling = new PlaneQ;
    outcircling = new PlaneQ;
    Plane *ip = 0, *op = 0;
    ok_take_off = 1;
    for(;;){
        delay( 10 );
        while(inair->notempty() && outcircling->isroom())
            outcircling->put( inair->get() );
        while(incoming->notempty() && incircling->isroom())
            incircling->put( incoming->get() );
        if (!ip ) ip = incircling->get();
        if( !op ) op = outcircling->get();
```

```
        if( ip ) {
            if( landing->isroom() ) {
                printf("flight %d arriving at %s\n",
                    ip->flt(), ip->to()->name() );
                landing->put( ip );
                ip = 0;
            }
            else {
                printf("flight %d delayed circling %s\n",
                    ip->flt(), ip->to()->name() );
            }
        }
        if( op ) {
            if( outgoing->isroom() ) {
                printf("flight %d leaving %s airspace\n",
                    op->flt(), op->from()->name() );
                outgoing->put( op );
                ok_take_off = 1;
                op = 0;
            }
            else {
                printf("flight %d delayed circling %s\n",
                    op->flt(), op->from()->name() );
                ok_take_off = 0;
            }
        }
    } // end for(;;)
}

int CentralControl::nairports = 0;
Airport **CentralControl::airports = 0;
urand *CentralControl::acity = 0;
```

```
CentralControl::CentralControl() {

    const int n = 10;
    nairports = n;
    acity = new urand ( 0, n-1 );
    static char *nms[ n ] = {
        "New York", "Newark", "Chicago",
        "Denver", "Columbus", "Austin",
        "Dallas", "San Francisco", "Portland",
        "San Jose",
    };
    airports = new Airport*[n];
    for( int i = 0; i < n; i++ ) {
        airports[ i ] =
            new Airport(new PlaneQ,new PlaneQ,i,nms[i]);
    }

    // give each airport some planes
    urand nplanes( 20, 40 );
    for( i = 0; i < n; i++ ) {
        Airport *port = airports[ i ];
        for( int m = nplanes.draw(); m;  m-- )
            port->onground->put( new Plane( 0, port ) );
    }

    // direct air traffic between airports
    // schedule new flights from empty airports
    for(;;) {
        delay( 10 );
        for( i = 0; i < n; i++ ) {
            Airport *port = airports[ i ];
            Plane *p = port->outgoing->get();
            if( p )
                if( p->to()->incoming->isroom() )
                    p->to()->incoming->put( p );
                else {
                    printf("flight %d crashed",
                        p->flt() );
                    delete p;
                }
```

```
            if( !port->onground->notempty() ) {
               port->onground->put(new Plane(0,port));
            }
         }
      } // end for(;;)
}

AirControl::~AirControl() {
    while( incircling->notempty()
           && incoming->notempty() )
      thistask->delay( 10 );
    Plane *p;
    while( p = outcircling->get() )
       incircling->put( p );
    while( incircling->notempty() )
       thistask->delay( 10 );
    cancel( 0 );
}

GroundControl::GroundControl( PlaneQ *takingoff,
                PlaneQ *onground ) {
    urand n( 10, 30 );
    Plane *p = 0;
    for(;;){
        delay( n.draw() );
        if( !p ) p = onground->get();
        if( p ) {
           if( takingoff->isroom() ) {
               p->reschedule(); // set new destination
               printf("flight %d leaving %s gate\n",
                       p->flt(), p->from()->name() );
               takingoff->put( p );
               p = 0;
             } else
               printf("flight %d delayed at %s gate\n",
                       p->flt(), p->from()->name() );
        }
    } // end for(;;)
}
```

```
int Plane::fltcount = 0;

void
Plane::reschedule() {
    origin = destination;
    destination = pickacity();
    start = sched::get_clock();
}

Airport::~Airport() {
    gcontrol->cancel(0);
    delete acontrol;
    while( landing->notempty() )
        thistask->delay( 10 );
    printf("%s Airport Closed\n", name() );
    cancel(0);
}

CentralControl::~CentralControl() {
    for( int i = 0; i < nairports ; i++ ) {
        delete airports[ i ];
    }
    printf("CentralControl Closed\n");
    cancel( 0 );
}

main() {
    CentralControl *ccp = new CentralControl;
    thistask->delay( 5000 );
    delete ccp;
    thistask->resultis(0);
}
```

☐

Exercise 7-8. The `ResourceHandle` abstract base class simply maintains all the active resources on a list, and provides the means to activate the virtual destructor for each active resource.

```cpp
class ResourceHandle {
  protected:
    ResourceHandle();
  public:
    virtual ~ResourceHandle() = 0;
  protected:
    void *operator new( size_t )
        { return 0; }
    void operator delete( void * )
        {}
  private:
    static ResourceHandle *latest;  // head of resource list
    ResourceHandle *prev;  // previous resource on list
    static void release(); // release all resources
    friend void recover(); // only routine allowed to release
};

ResourceHandle *ResourceHandle::latest = 0;

ResourceHandle::ResourceHandle()
    : prev( latest )
    { latest = this; }

ResourceHandle::~ResourceHandle()
    {}

void
ResourceHandle::release() {
    for( ResourceHandle *p = latest; p; p = p->prev )
        p->~ResourceHandle();
}

void
recover() {
    ResourceHandle::release();
    longjmp( main_loop_env, 1 );
}
```

The exception handling mechanism discussed in Chapter 8, if available on your C++ compiler, is generally a better alternative than hand-coded recovery. □

Exercise 7-10. We create a generic pointer type that is instantiated with the type of object to which it refers:

```
template <class Rtype>
class Hptr {
    Rtype *p;
  public:
    Hptr( Rtype *v = 0 )
        { p = v; }
    operator Rtype *()
        { return p; }
    Rtype &operator *() {
        check(p);
        return *p;
    }
    Rtype &operator[]( long i ) {
        check(p+i);
        return p[i];
    }
    Hptr &operator ++() {
        p++;
        return *this;
    }
    // etc. ...
};
```

Our generic pointer is implemented as a regular pointer to the type with which the generic pointer is instantiated. We supply all the usual arithmetic operations on pointers (although we show only prefix ++ above) by performing the operation on regular pointer in the representation. The operations * and [ ] check the pointer address, however, before dereferencing to ensure that it refers to free store.

The implementation of the routine that performs this check is highly dependent on the environment in which our pointer type is used. The Unix system call sbrk can be used to find the current bounds of free store.

```
static char *ilimit;
class HptrInit {// See Exercise 8-16.
  public:
    HptrInit() { ilimit = sbrk(0); }
};
```

```
static HptrInit init;

void
check( void *p ) {
    if( p < ilimit || p >= sbrk(0) )
        error();
}
```

Alternatively, greater efficiency and a measure of environment independence is possible if operators `new` and `delete` have been redefined. In this case, `new` and `delete` can maintain a list of starting and ending addresses of free store blocks, obviating the need for `check` to perform a system call each time a smart pointer is dereferenced.

Our pointer type as defined above can be instantiated with any type, so we can have safe heap pointers to predefined types like `char`s and `double`s as well as class types.

```
typedef Hptr<char> CHptr;
typedef Hptr<double> DHptr;

struct Pair {
    int i, j;
};
typedef Hptr<Pair> PHptr;
PHptr pub;
```

Our generic pointer does not provide an `operator ->` because `->` cannot be used with pointers to nonclass types. Therefore, to access a member of a `Pair` with a `PHptr`, we must use the syntax `(*pub).i` rather than `pub->i`. We could augment our generic pointer type to allow the `->` operator, but then it could no longer be instantiated with nonclass types. Alternatively, we could provide a second pointer type to be instantiated with class types only.

In providing the solution to this exercise, we have taken some liberties in interpreting the statement of the problem. We were to design a generic pointer that is guaranteed to point only to free store, but we have implemented a pointer that can only *reference* free store. The pointer can contain any address at all; the address contained in the pointer is only checked just before it is dereferenced with a `*` or `[]`.

This could be a problem, because we have provided a conversion operator that allows conversion to the corresponding regular pointer type.

```
char *strcpy( char *, const char * );
CHptr s;
char *t;
strcpy( s, t );
```

The conversion could allow the address contained in the pointer to be used even if it did not refer to free store.

We could approach this problem by getting rid of the conversion operator, but this would reduce the utility of our type because we could no longer use objects of the type as actual arguments and operands to existing functions and operators that are declared to work with the corresponding regular pointer types. Our generic pointer type would not be integrated into the predefined type system.

Alternatively, we could assure that the value of the pointer always referred to free store by checking the value after each initialization, assignment, and arithmetic operation, instead of on dereferencing. This would (occasionally) prevent our pointer type from being used in any algorithm that attempts to reference past the end of a data structure if the data structure is at the end of free store.

```
int
strlen2( CHptr s ) {
    // return length of string, including '\0'
    CHptr t = s;
    while( *t++ );
    return t-s;
}
```

Since t eventually contains an address past the end of the character string to which s refers, it could conceivably be a non-freestore address.

Is it possible to say which of these approaches is correct, or are there situations in which each of these approaches is preferred to the others? □

Exercise 7-14.

```
class Delegand;

class Delegator {
   Delegand *delegand;
 public:
   // Delegator's own operations
   void op1();
   // ...
   // Everything else is forwarded to Delegand
   Delegand *operator ->()
      { return delegand; }
};

class Delegand {
 public:
   // Operations shared by Delegator and Delegand
   int op1();
   // ...
};
```

Under this scheme, any `Delegator` operation accessed with a `.` operator is a member of `Delegator`, and any operation accessed with a `->` operator is forwarded to the corresponding `Delegand` object.

```
extern Delegator d, *dp, &dr;
d.op1();  // member of Delegator
d->op1(); // forwarded
dp->op1();   // member of Delegator
dr->op1();   // forwarded
```

☐

Exercise 7-15. An object with a private destructor cannot be allocated as a static or as an automatic, since the compiler would then attempt to invoke the private destructor. For heap allocation, it is necessary to provide another way to delete the object and invoke the destructor.

```
class HeapOnly {
  public:
   HeapOnly();
   void Delete()
      { delete this; }
  private:
   ~HeapOnly();
};
```

A type that uses this technique is often used in combination with a type whose objects can only be allocated on the stack or as statics. The heap-resident ''implementation'' objects are reference counted by the stack-resident ''handle'' objects.

```
class Impl {
    Impl()
       : refs( 1 ) {}
    ~Impl()
       {}
    int refs;
    void func1();
    int func2();
    // ...
    friend class Handle;
};

class Handle {
  public:
   Handle()
      : impl( new Impl ) {}
   Handle( const Handle &h )
      : impl( h.impl )
      { impl->refs++; }
   ~Handle()
      { if( !--impl->refs ) delete impl; }
```

```
      Handle &operator =( const Handle &h ) {
          if( this != &h ) {
              if( !--impl->refs )
                  delete impl;
              impl = h.impl;
              impl->refs++;
          }
          return *this;
      }
      Impl *operator ->()
          { return impl; }
  protected:
    Impl *impl;
    void *operator new( size_t )
        { return 0; }
    void operator delete( void * )
        {}
  };
```

□

Exercise 8-1. For simplicity and better likelihood of correctness, we have the message buffer object control all the operations on its implementation buffers. Buffer overflow is not an error; the message is simply truncated. However, we provide users the ability to determine if a message has been truncated and to specify whether or not buffers are to be reallocated and copied on overflow.

```
class MsgBuf {
  public:
    MsgBuf( size_t length = 81 );
    MsgBuf( const MsgBuf & );
    ~MsgBuf();
    MsgBuf &operator =( const MsgBuf & );  // deep
    MsgBuf &operator =( const char * ); // deep
    MsgBuf &operator <<( char );
    MsgBuf &operator <<( int );
    MsgBuf &operator <<( unsigned int );
    MsgBuf &operator <<( long );
    MsgBuf &operator <<( unsigned long );
    MsgBuf &operator <<( float );
    MsgBuf &operator <<( double );
```

```
      MsgBuf &operator <<( const char * );
      MsgBuf &operator <<( const MsgBuf & );
      MsgBuf &operator <<( void (*manip)( MsgBuf & ) );
      operator const char *() const; // shallow
      int length() const;     // includes '\0'
      int maxlen() const;     // current size of buffer
      void make_expandable();        // realloc on overflow
      void make_fixed_size();        // don't realloc (default)
      int expanded() const;      // buf was realloced
      int overflowed() const;        // buf overflowed realloc
      friend void clear_buf( MsgBuf & );  // a manipulator
    private:
      size_t bmax; // length of this buffer
      char *b;  // the message buffer
      size_t len;  // current first unused index
      char realloc;   // flags permission to expand buffer
      char overflow;  // flags buffer overflow
      int expand();   // realloc buffer
  };

  inline
  MsgBuf::operator const char *() const
      { return b; }

  inline int
  MsgBuf::length() const
      { return len+1; }

  inline int
  MsgBuf::maxlen() const
      { return bmax; }

  inline void
  MsgBuf::make_expandable()
      { realloc = 1; }

  inline void
  MsgBuf::make_fixed_size()
      { realloc = 0; }
```

```
inline int
MsgBuf::expanded() const
    { return realloc ? realloc - 1 : 0; }

inline int
MsgBuf::overflowed() const
    { return overflow; }
```

The default constructor and destructor ensure that the `MsgBuf` object is initialized to a stable state and properly cleaned up.

```
MsgBuf::MsgBuf( size_t length )
    : bmax( length < 1 ? 1 : length ), b( new char[bmax] ),
        len( 0 ), realloc( 0 ), overflow( 0 )
    { b[0] = '\0'; }

MsgBuf::~MsgBuf()
    { delete b; }
```

The assignment operators clean up the existing buffer and make a copy of the argument to initialize the new buffer. For efficiency, the existing buffer is reused if it is large enough.

```
MsgBuf &
MsgBuf::operator =( const MsgBuf &m ) {
    return *this = m.b;
}
```

```
MsgBuf &
MsgBuf::operator =( const char *s ) {
    if( s != b ) {
        int slen = strlen( s );
        while( bmax < slen )
            if( !expand() ) {
                my_strncpy( b, s, bmax );
                overflow++;
                return *this;
            }
        my_strncpy( b, s, bmax );
        len = slen;
    }
    return *this;
}
```

The implementation of the character string insertion operator is straightforward.

```
MsgBuf &
MsgBuf::operator <<( const char *s ) {
    if( !s )
        return *this;
    int n = strlen( s );
    if( bmax-len > n ) {
stuffit:
        my_strncpy( b+len, s, bmax-len );
        len += n;
    }
```

```
        else if( realloc )
           if( expand() )
              goto stuffit;
           else {
              // Copy as much as possible, anyway...
      stuffsome:
              my_strncpy( b+len, s, bmax-len );
              overflow++;
           }
        else
           goto stuffsome;
        return *this;
     }
```

For convenience, the other insertion operators can be implemented, at least initially, in terms of the character string insertion operator. Later, a more efficient implementation may be required.

```
     MsgBuf &
     MsgBuf::operator <<( int i ) {
        char integer[ 12 ];
        sprintf( integer, "%d", i );
        return *this << integer;
     }
```

The private `expand` function handles the implementation buffer expansion on overflow.

```
     int
     MsgBuf::expand() {
        char *newb;
        size_t newmax = (3*bmax)/2;   // 50% increase
        newb = new char[ newmax ];
        my_strncpy( newb, b, newmax );
        b = newb;
        bmax = newmax;
        realloc++;
        delete b;
        return 1;
     }
```

Note that we did not attempt to catch a certain class of errors, including failure of `operator new`, stack overflow, and asynchronous events like user interrupts. We must assume that these error conditions are handled through the proper functioning and communication of the systems involved. For example, on failure, `operator new` may raise an exception to be caught by the application. The participation of `MsgBuf` is not required for correct handling of such error conditions. `MsgBuf` may assist in recovery, however, by requiring that `MsgBuf` objects be allocated on the stack, thus ensuring that any memory allocated by a `MsgBuf` will be freed when its destructor is actived by the exception handling mechanism. □

Exercise 8-2. The `expand` function encapsulates the semantics of buffer reallocation, so we make it virtual to allow customization by derived classes.

```
class MsgBuf {
    // ...
    virtual int expand();
    // ...
};

class PanicOnOvflMsgBuf : public MsgBuf {
    int expand();
};

int
PanicOnOvflMsgBuf::expand() {
    panic();
    return 0;
}
```

□

Exercise 8-8. We assume we have available a function that rounds a complex value:

```
complex round( complex );
```

All we have to do is supply the appropriate applicator.

```
inline complex
operator +( complex val, complex (*manip)(complex) )
    { return manip( val ); }
```

Providing the same functionality for integer expressions requires a different approach. Recall that a user-defined operator must have at least one class type argument. Since `int`s do not have class type, we have to make the other argument to `operator +` have class type. Here is one way:

```
int int_round( int );

class ROUND {};
ROUND iround;

inline int
operator +( int ival, ROUND /* dummy */ )
    { return int_round( ival ); }
```

☐

Exercise 8-11. Since `SortedCollection` already has a way of applying a function to each element of the collection in the correct order, we use that. Unfortunately, the `apply` function can only take an argument of type `void (*)(Etype)`, so we must devise a way to pass the `ostream` to the `apply` function.

```
static ostream *oarg;

void
print( Etype e ) {
    *oarg << e;
    *oarg << " ";
}

ostream &
operator <<( ostream &out, SortedCollection &sc ) {
    out << "{ ";
    oarg = &out; // kludge...
    apply( print );
    out << "}";
    return out;
}
```

What are the potential problems with this solution? How would you solve it if you could change the interface to `SortedCollection`? How would a control abstraction type help? ☐

Exercise 8-16. One solution is to create an initialization type whose constructor initializes the library. We declare a static object of the initialization type in the library source, *not* in the header file!

```
// In library source...
class LibInit {
  public:
    LibInit() {
        // lib init code...
    }
    ~LibInit() {
        // lib cleanup code...
    }
};
static LibInit init;
```

The implicit constructor invocation for the static initialization object will initialize the library at the start of execution. Conversely, the destructor invocation will perform any required cleanup before the end of execution.

Alternatively, a static `LibInit` object can be defined in the library header file, and a counter declared as a static data member can be used to control the initialization and cleanup.

```
// In library header...
class LibInit {
  public:
    LibInit() {
        if( !users++ ) {
            // lib init code...
        }
    }
    ~LibInit() {
        if( !--users ) {
            // lib cleanup code...
        }
    }
  private:
    static long users;
};
static LibInit init;

// In library source...
long LibInit::users = 0;
```

This second mechanism has the advantage of having the ability to delay the initialization of a library until other libraries, upon which it depends, have been initialized.

Note that static objects will still be subject to runtime initialization, and the order in which the static objects in different files are initialized is undefined. Static objects of a class with a constructor will be initialized during runtime initialization, but can generally be reinitialized through the use of an explicit destructor call and placement new, as described in Chapter 7. Such static objects may have to take special pains to avoid reinitialization by a default runtime initialization after being initialized through the LibInit mechanism.

One approach is to accept the default runtime initialization and perform more general initialization after main has started execution.

The Init class below is used as a base class of any library initialization type that depends on the prior initialization of another library. Init constructs a cross-translation-unit dependency graph at static initialization time, then performs a topological sort of the Init objects and executes each Init object's virtual ctor function in that topological order. The Init objects are invoked in a correct inverse order to activate the virtual dtor function at the end of execution.

```cpp
class Init {
  protected:
    Init( Init *a = 0, Init *b = 0,
        Init *c = 0, Init *d = 0 );
    virtual void ctor() = 0;
    virtual void dtor() = 0;
  public:
    virtual ~Init();
    static void globalCtor();
    static void globalDtor();
  private:
    static Init *head;  // global list of Init objects
    Init *next;       // next Init object in list
    Init *depend[5];// dependency list
    char initted;       // flags init done for node
    char cleanedup;     // flags cleanup done for node
    void dfsCtor();
    void dfsDtor();
  protected:
    // no heap allocation
    void *operator new( size_t );
    void operator delete( void * );
```

```
        private:
          // no copying
          void operator =( Init & );
          Init( Init & );
    };
```

Classes derived from `Init` generally have a single static object. The constructor and destructor for such derived type objects will be invoked at runtime static initialization time, and typically will do nothing or will prepare the object for its later initialization function. Since any library upon which it depends may not be initialized, it may not begin initialization of its own library.

After runtime static initialization is complete, the static member function `Init::globalCtor` is invoked (typically in main) to cause the virtual `ctor` function of each `Init` object to be called to perform the library initialiazation. Similarly, the static function `Init::globalDtor` is invoked to activate each `Init` object's virtual `dtor` function to clean up the library.

```
    Init *Init::head = 0;

    Init::Init( Init *a, Init *b, Init *c, Init *d )
        : initted( 0 ), cleanedup( 0 ) {
        depend[0] = a;
        depend[1] = b;
        depend[2] = c;
        depend[3] = d;
        depend[4] = 0;

        // put this Init on a global list
        next = head;
        head = this;
    }

    Init::~Init()
        {}
```

```
void
Init::globalCtor() {
    // there's no guarantee that the dependency graph
    // is connected, so check every node
    for( Init *p = head; p; p = p->next )
        p->dfsCtor();
}

void
Init::globalDtor() {
    for( Init *p = head; p; p = p->next )
        p->dfsDtor();
}

void
Init::dfsCtor() {
    if( !initted ) {
        initted = 1;
        for( int i = 0; depend[i]; i++ )
            if( !depend[i]->initted )
                depend[i]->dfsCtor();
        ctor();
    }
}

void
Init::dfsDtor() {
    if( !cleanedup ) {
        dtor();
        cleanedup = 1;
        for( int i = 0; depend[i]; i++ )
            if( !depend[i]->cleanedup )
                depend[i]->dfsDtor();
    }
}
```

Rather than use a varargs list and the difficulties it entails, we allow no more that four dependencies for a given subsystem. If this is too restrictive, the user can "cascade" multiple `Init` objects together to achieve the same effect. ☐

Index